THE STAFFORDSHIRE WAY

Les Lumsdon and Chris Rushton

Published by Sigma Leisure – an imprint of
Sigma Press, 1 South Oak Lane, Wilmslow, Cheshire SK9 6AR, England.

British Library Cataloguing in Publication Data
A CIP record for this book is available from the British Library.

ISBN: 1-85058-315-3

Typesetting and Design by: Sigma Press, Wilmslow, Cheshire.

Maps by: Pam Upchurch

Text photographs: Chris Rushton

Cover photograph: Chris Rushton

Printed by: Manchester Free Press

General Disclaimer

Whilst every effort has been made to ensure that the information given in this book is correct, neither the publisher nor the author accept any responsibility for any inaccuracy.

CONTENTS

INTRODUCTION

SECTION 1:
A GUIDE TO THE STAFFORDSHIRE WAY

SECTION 2:
TEN LOCAL WALKS BASED ON THE STAFFORDSHIRE WAY

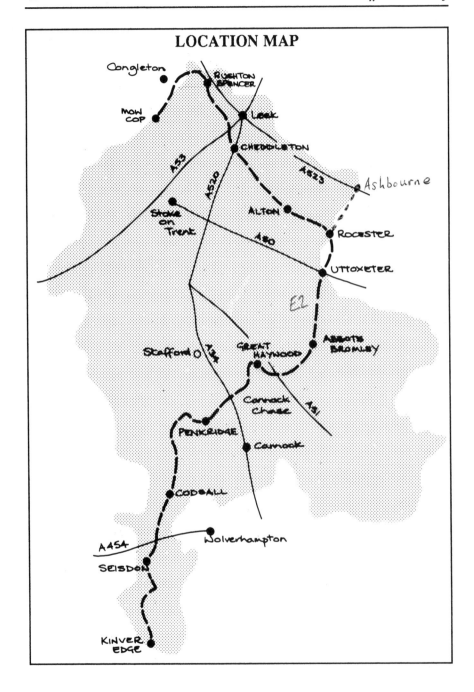

THE STAFFORDSHIRE WAY

For a long while, The Staffordshire Way was little known. Maybe that is how it is with routes which seemingly begin and end at out-of-the-way places, traversing a countryside that is neither mountainous nor coastal. Yet this is a long distance path which unfolds powerful images of old England. The starting point, Mow Cop, was the scene of momentous religious gatherings during the last century. What would it have been like to stand beneath the folly with thousands of others listening to the driving passion of Primitive Methodism? There's still a stirring sense of history on this windswept hillside, currents of past and present, as you stand looking towards the Cheshire plains below.

Ancient Parish Churches

So it is throughout the route. The path delivers you to ancient parish churches, industrial relics and former rural resorts. It passes by handsome Georgian farmhouses, steadfast on the land, and village greens adorned with cottage, inn and shop. Each sleepy location tells its own story. The romanticism of Rudyard Lake and the association of this place with "Rudyard" Kipling, the portrayal of Rocester as "Rosseter" in Eliot's "Adam Bede", or the intriguing cave houses at Kinver are all to be explored on The Way.

Pockets of Landscape

It is a fascinating route in other respects. The diversity of the landscape and farming comes as a surprise to those who are not familiar with Staffordshire. From the gritstone edges of the northern section to the lowland pastures of South Staffordshire, the Way manages to weave between several pockets of landscape. There are high wooded bluffs leading down to the watery meadows of the Churnet and Dove, attractive to wildlife and a pleasure to the eye. The wooded slopes of Cannock Chase, that ancient Royal hunting ground exploited by humans throughout the centuries, create a very different landscape. Here recent coniferous plantations grow opposite long standing oak woodlands such as Brocton Coppice. There are also large tracts of heathland, home to a variety of butterflies and moths and a host of other insects.

The Way then descends to gently undulating farmland, intensively cultivated for the Midlands markets. The highlight has to be South Staffordshire's impressive parklands, ingeniously contrived by the great gardeners of the time, parklands which form part of major estates such as Chillington and Enville. The Staffordshire Way ends triumphantly as it begins on a high bluff. The views are inspiration enough to recall on the homeward journey.

Celebration of Villages

Another endearing feature of the route is the pattern of villages through which it passes. In several respects The Way invites the walker to celebrate village life away from the bustle of urban roads. Many of the communities *en route* offer accommodation, inns and shops, the necessities of long distance walking. Several are also home to visitor attractions such as the Flint Mill and Railway Centre at Cheddleton, the Falconry near Kingsley, magnificent Shugborough Hall at Great Haywood or the enterprising vineyard at Halfpenny Green. It is the combination of village and attraction that breaks up the route. In the southern sections, it comes closer to urban areas but nevertheless maintains a distinctly rural path. This is a joy for those who seek to escape from busy towns.

Staffordshire County Council

The entire route is 92 miles in length, a good mileage on which to base a holiday. Staffordshire County Council devised and developed The Way in the late 1970s through to 1983. This must have been a difficult task for those involved in the tortuous negotiations with landowners and different authorities on the route, determining an acceptable path to all concerned. Our hats go off to their endeavours for it is now a very useful recreational facility for local people and visitors alike.

During the past ten years The Way has grown in popularity almost as a result of word of mouth recommendation. The Way has been promoted in leaflets and books produced by the County Council on the route itself. Unlike some National Trails it does not suffer from the problems of heavy use and consequent erosion. There are a few places where the locality, rather than The Way itself, brings larger numbers of casual walkers particularly on Sunday afternoons, places like The Cloud, Rudyard, Alton, The Chase and Kinver Edge. Otherwise the route is relatively quiet – especially if you choose to walk mid-week or on a Saturday.

Using This Book

The Staffordshire Way is well waymarked (yellow or blue marker with Stafford Knot emblem) in places and less so on others, so a guidebook comes in handy. This book offers a route description for those wishing to walk the length of the County. Its main purpose, however, is for ramblers who wish to use the Staffordshire Way for day walking or as part of a circular ramble from a particular locality. There are 10 sections, each offering a day's walk and exploration. These are supplemented by suggestions for local walks and ten circular rambles written up from villages on the Way. Thus, the book is meant to be a companion to those who wish to use the route for local walking as well as the person taking a short break or week's holiday.

Planning Ahead

The rambler who aims to walk a good section of the route should plan a rough itinerary and book accommodation through the respective tourist information offices mentioned below. The Guide mentions shops and pubs and along most of the route. You will not have far to walk to buy provisions or find a refreshment stop. Staffordshire County Council produces a leaflet entitled 'The Staffordshire Way" which lists current accommodation availability. This book lists places where accommodation may be found rather than actual addresses to contact, as these tend to change more frequently than reprints of books!

Clothing

While the Staffordshire Way does not follow high ground for most of its route it is important to have the right kit before setting off on your adventure. While shorts and a Tee shirt might suffice on a warm Summer's day be prepared for colder weather and pack a jumper even for day walking. More importantly, ensure that you have waterproof garments such as a breathable cagoule and overtrousers. It is no fun walking in the rain without protection.

While some prefer trainers, the authors recommend comfortable "worn in" boots and socks, ones that fit! There is nothing worse than sore feet and blisters on a holiday ramble, so look after those little tootsies. It is also worthwhile taking a small first aid kit and a drink and snack in a knapsack or rucksack just in case.

Pace

A seasoned long distance walker might achieve 15 to 20 miles easily on The Staffordshire Way. Many of us will want to savour the route, admire the views, take a meal at lunch-time or call into an attraction. Allow time to enjoy the good things in life! It will not only enhance your break but also gives something back to the local community. Estimate a steady 2.5 miles per hour in addition to stops. This means that most sections of the route will offer a comfortable day's walking say between half past nine and six in the evening. There are quite a few stiles to cross throughout, except on the towpath sections, but otherwise there are very few hard climbs or descents.

Obstructions and Diversions

The authors found no obstructions on the route but encountered minor diversions. These result from remedial work where bridges or the like have collapsed and are well-signposted by the County Council.

Information

The following information will help you to plan your route whether it is a day walk or a week's tour. We have not included listings of accommodation as very often details change within the timespan of a book. Tourist Information Offices (known to book accommodation) listed below will be able to provide you with up to the minute information.

Tourist Information Centres

Hanley
> Potteries Shopping Centre
> Quadrant Road
> Stoke-on-Trent
> Phone: (0782) 284600

Congleton (in Cheshire)
> Town Hall
> High Street
> Congleton
> Phone: (0260) 271095

Leek
> Market Place
> Leek
> Phone: (0538) 381000

Stafford
> The Ancient High House
> Greengate Street
> Stafford
> Phone: (0785) 40204

Kinver
> Travellers Joy
> 47 High St
> Kinver
> Phone: (0384) 872940

Wolverhampton (West Midlands)
> 18 Queen Square
> Wolverhampton
> Phone: (0902) 312051

Public Transport

The authors endorse the "Countrygoer" concept which encourages the use of public transport into the countryside rather than taking a car. The entire route was researched using buses and trains. This is quite easy on most sections of the route as many of the villages and towns enjoy a reasonable level of service (say 6 or 7 buses a day). Wherever possible, public transport information has been included. In this respect Staffordshire Busline is invaluable as it is a one-stop information service on all bus companies running near to The Way.

The Staffordshire Busline telephone number is (0785) 223344. This "hotline" provides an invaluable service. It is available Monday to Friday and Saturday mornings.

The main public transport links serving The Staffordshire Way can be summarised as follows:

Mow Cop: A good daily service from Hanley allowing ready access to the start of the route.

Congleton: There is a pleasant walk linking Congleton railway station with the Mow Cop Trail. Congleton enjoys an hourly to two hourly service on Mondays to Saturdays. The Sunday service is much more limited.

Timbersbrook: Limited Mondays to Saturdays bus service from Congleton.

Rushton: Enjoys a daily service, the 201 bus between Manchester and Derby. This allows opportunities for linear walks between Rushton and Leek every day of the week.

Longsdon: There is a regular service (half-hourly for the most part) on Mondays to Saturdays from Leek and Hanley but a less frequent timetable on Sundays.

Cheddleton: This village has an hourly service from Hanley and Leek.

Kingsley: Regular service (half-hourly for the most part) on Mondays to Saturdays to and from Hanley.

Alton: Five or six buses to or from Cheadle (connections from Hanley) as well as Uttoxeter on Mondays to Saturdays.

Rocester: Approximately 10 buses between Rocester and Uttoxeter on Mondays to Saturdays allowing easy access to The Staffordshire Way.

Uttoxeter: The Staffordshire Way passes by Uttoxeter railway station which is served daily by trains from Derby and Stoke-on-Trent.

Abbots Bromley: Very limited service on Mondays to Saturdays from Stafford and Uttoxeter. Makes it more difficult to enjoy a linear walk from here.

Colwich: Regular daily service (half-hourly for the most part) to Stafford.

Great Haywood: Regular daily service (half hourly for the most part, hourly on Sundays).

Brocton: Regular daily service to Stafford.

Penkridge: Train service on Mondays to Saturdays between Stafford and Wolverhampton. Daily bus service from Stafford and Wolverhampton making Penkridge a good starting point for a linear walk.

Brewood: Regular daily bus service to Wolverhampton.

Codsall: Daily train service to Codsall. Regular daily bus service (half hourly mainly) to Wolverhampton.

Trescott: Regular service on Mondays to Saturdays to Wolverhampton. Limited Sunday service.

Seisdon: Limited Monday to Saturday service to Wolverhampton.

Enville: Very limited service.

Kinver: Regular daily service (mainly hourly) to Stourbridge and Cradley Heath.

Linear Walks

The Staffordshire Way lends itself to several linear walks using public transport. In particular the following are easily accessible day walks.

Route Section:	*Mileage*
Mow Cop to Rushton	11 miles
Rushton to Longsdon	7 miles
Longsdon to Kingsley	7 miles
Alton to Uttoxeter	7 miles
Uttoxeter to Colwich	14 miles
Great Haywood to Penkridge	8 miles
Penkridge to Brewood	9 miles
Brewood to Codsall	4 miles
Seisdon to Kinver	12 miles

Other Long Distance Paths

The Staffordshire Way links with the following paths:

Mow Cop: The South Cheshire Way
Rushton: Brindley's Trail and The Gritstone Trail
Cannock Chase: Heart of England Way
Kinver: Worcestershire Way and North Worcestershire Path

SECTION 1: THE ROUTE

The first part of the book, Section 1, describes The Staffordshire Way in a series of 10 day walks of varying length. They offer considerable scope for those seeking a day's walking and also for walkers who wish to spend a few days sauntering along the route.

SECTION 2: CIRCULAR WALKS

In addition to the main route, there are ten local walks, described in Section 2. These are ideal for sampling the many delightful aspects of The Staffordshire Way, perhaps before you tackle the entire route.

SECTION 1:
A GUIDE TO THE STAFFORDSHIRE WAY

MOW COP TO RUSHTON SPENCER

Route: Mow Cop – Nick i' th' Hill – Timbersbrook – The Cloud – Ravensbrook – Rushton Spencer

Distance: 9.5 miles

Map: O.S. Pathfinder Sheets 792 Kidsgrove and Leek and 776 Congleton

Start: The Folly at Mow Cop (Grid Reference 857574)

Access: Mow Cop enjoys a regular bus service from Hanley. Car drivers might wish to travel on the A34 to Scholar Green, turning right and right again from Mow Cop as signposted. There is a car park at the folly or on street parking nearby.

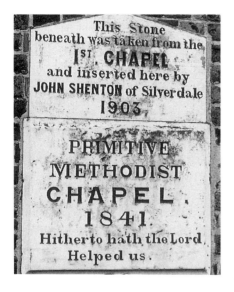

This Stone beneath was taken from the 1st CHAPEL and inserted here by JOHN SHENTON of Silverdale 1903

PRIMITIVE METHODIST CHAPEL 1841

Hitherto hath the Lord Helped us.

Mow Cop

This most unlikely hilltop quarrying settlement became the birthplace of Primitive Methodism during the last century. A local carpenter, Hugh Bourne and other local speakers held camp meetings in and around the Mow Cop folly during the early decades of the last century. It seems hard to believe that 10000 or more passionate religious supporters would walk miles to this windswept hillside to hear the readings of the break-away group. It is a clear indication of their commitment to a faith that spread through many industrialising settlements. Primitive methodism grew from strength to strength throughout the following decades and there are dozens of chapels in the area built during the 19th century. The movement was reunited with the Methodist church during the austere years of the early 1930s.

One other curious feature worthy of mention is the Old Man of Mow. It is less well-known than the folly built in 1754 for local landowner Randle Wilbraham to enhance his view from nearby Rode Hall. The Old Man, shown in the picture below, is a curious remnant of rock left standing by quarrymen, an early piece of creative sculpture for the rock really does present a picture of an old man looking across the Cheshire Plain. And what an exceptional view he has.

Timbersbrook

Timbersbrook owes its existence to a fast flowing brook which was dammed to provide water power for a mill. There are scant remains of the complex surviving in the hamlet near to the picnic site. Timbersbrook has always been a local favourite with cyclists and walkers and, until recent years, there was a little cafe offering refreshment. That no longer exists but it is as well to take a breather here before the climb up to Bosley Cloud.

Bosley Cloud

This high standing Gritstone Edge is evidence of the divide between the harder grits and the softer sandstones of the Cheshire Plain below. Like Mow Cop it is a well-known feature hereabouts and is particularly popular with those who enjoy wild bilberries. Now in National Trust ownership, The Cloud is a place to be with a picnic when there's a fine summer or autumn sunset as the views are delicious. In earlier times, the edges have been quarried for local use and many of the strange outcrops have been given names such as Bully Thrumble. In the foreground you can see Bosley Aqueduct and Bosley railway viaduct. Both these structures were built using stone hewn from these slopes.

The Cloud must be one of the highlights of the Staffordshire Way and is well worth savouring unless there happens to be a gale force wind. Then, caution should be exercised.

Accommodation and Refreshment:

There are several pubs in Mow Cop, of which the authors' preference is the Cheshire View, 5 minutes walk from the folly down the precipitous Station Road. There is a well stocked village stores near to the folly along High Street.

There's also the Castle public house just off the route where the Staffordshire Way crosses the Biddulph to Congleton road. Unfortunately, refreshment will not be found in Timbersbrook these days.

Accommodation is available in The Potteries and Congleton.

The Walk

(1) Start at the monument at Mow Cop. Facing the folly, head slightly left up the bank as signposted. This leads to a track between buildings, and swiftly to Castle Road. Turn right and then go almost immediately left up a shaded track between bungalows.

(2) The track skirts heather-clad ground in front of The Old Man of Mow, a solitary pillar of rock reaching towards the sky and said to resemble the features of an old man. The views over the Cheshire Plain are panoramic in the very sense of the word, stretching from the dark hills of Clwyd to Greater Manchester and Merseyside.

(3) Pass a cottage to a junction where a path to the left is signposted to Acker's Crossing. Follow the track right to a cross roads. Turn left here along a narrow road with glimpses across to The Potteries including the tall block of flats in Hanley known locally as Hanley Castle.

(4) At the Congleton Road, cross to face the traffic. This section is unpleasant as too many cars pass at high speed, but the view across to Biddulph and Lask Edge offers some compensation. Biddulph church and Biddulph Grange can also be seen. The latter is a most unusual Victorian Garden, featuring layouts which depict different parts of the world, such as the Italian or Chinese sections. It has largely been restored, although this must be an everlasting task as the garden evolves as a visitor attraction of the 21st century. The National Trust administers the property and, given that it is only a five minute bus ride up the road, you should seriously contemplate a visit.

(5) Pass the turning to the right, Mow Lane. The road descends Pot bank. Part way down keep ahead along a worn track as the road bends left. This track continues along the ridge then curves right to descend to a gap, known appropriately as Nick i' th' Hill. This out-of-the way settlement, seen in the photograph on the next page, is at the end of a "No Through Road" and nestles around a small Non-Conformist chapel.

The Way dips to Nick i' th' Hill . . .

(6) Turn right at the road to pass by houses. The road turns left but you continue ahead along a rough track which curves left and right. There is woodland to the left and a cottage to the right in what at first sight appears to be a very quiet corner of the world.

(7) Continue straight on, as signposted, by a fenced building. Brace yourself, for there are dogs here and they make their presence known. The path proceeds through the wood, a tranquil location to soothe the nerves. The narrow path twists between bracken and broken branches to exit by way of a stile beneath a tall oak.

(8) Head slightly right along a path beneath a slight ridge in the field, complete with rabbit burrows. At the marker post (with a farm on the right), turn right to a stile. Cross it and turn right to walk down the track. Pass the farm and then follow the track as it winds down to beneath the old railway trackbed, at one time the Biddulph branch of the North Staffordshire Railway. This railway, known affec-

tionately as "The Knotty" comprised an intensive network of passenger and freight lines branching out from The Potteries into Staffordshire and Cheshire. The headquarters of this august organisation was the handsome Jacobean style building which is now Inter-City's Stoke-on-Trent station. Most of the upper part of the building is occupied by Staffordshire University, and the main lecture theatre retains an impressive charm from the boardroom days of a century ago. There are many reminders about the railway in the vicinity, including drainage inspection covers which still have the N.S.R. identity forged into them. Once under the bridge go left over a stile and up steps to the old trackbed. Turn right.

(9) Follow this linear path for nearly a mile to the overbridge crossing the A527 (where there are steps down to the Castle pub, and buses for Congleton and Biddulph). Otherwise, continue along the path to cross over Reade's Lane. Proceed for approximately one quarter of a mile. Cross a narrow underpass and look out for a path leading off right from the right of the wooden barrier.

(10) This leads down steps to a stile where the path is signposted to Brookhouse. Cross the stile and keep ahead along the old railway boundary to the corner of the field. Turn right and the path keeps ahead through two fields to approach a farm. Please pass through the yard with consideration and turn right on Brook Lane. After 50 metres turn left as signposted beneath a garden to a gap stile. The Way continues ahead through four fields, at first by an old hedge line, then curving right to a stile. The path dips and continues ahead to another stile above the Timbersbrook. The path drops to a footbridge then winds around alongside the mill to a track. Keep ahead to Weathercock Lane, a reminder that rural communities always have an eye on the weather.

(11) Those wishing to finish a walk here should turn right for the car park at Timbersbrook, a possible cut-off point. Buses to Congleton leave from the shelter between the car park entrance and the crossroads. Otherwise turn left and pass houses on the left. Go next right up Acorn Lane, a superb green track lined with oaks. This joins a road by a lovely old cottage.

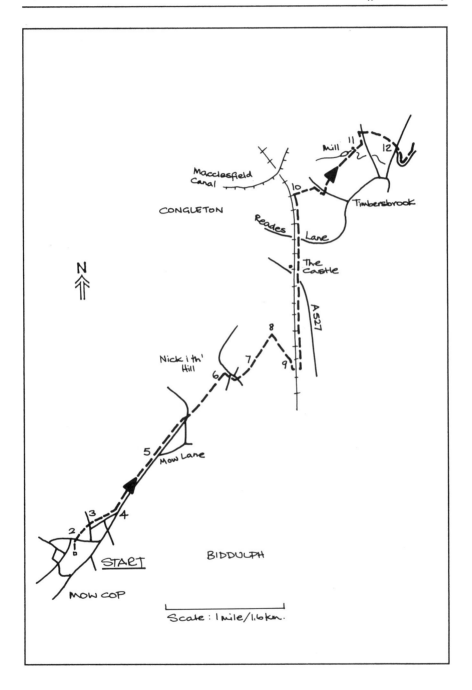

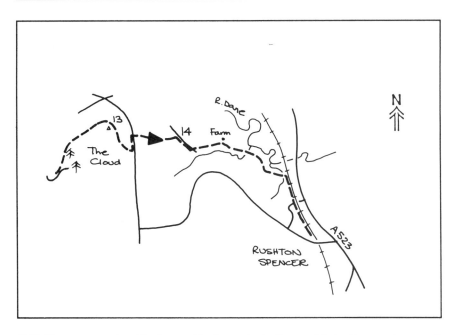

(12) Cross over to climb up Gosberryhole Lane. Note the spring well by the road sign. The track rises past Folly Cottage allowing a view back to Congleton Edge. Just beyond go left up a well-worn path by the National Trust sign. The path leads to the wood's edge, but keep left up the heather-clad hillside. The path steepens and becomes a scramble through rocks as it rises to the trig point at the summit. The views across Cheshire and Western Peakland are exquisite. This must be a place to rest awhile and sip wine with the Gods.

(13) From Bosley Cloud the path descends through heather until a set of steep ugly steps drop to a track. Go left to a metalled road. Bear left again and as the road begins to descend go right up the roadside bank to a stile hidden by scrub. Cross it and follow the field's edge along the hillside, crossing wooden planks where the ground is very wet. Cross a wooden stile and proceed ahead along the top of the field to another stile. Once over bear slightly left through a birch wood. This thins to a few straggling hawthorns as the path loses height. The path comes to the remaining posts of a grubbed hedge. Cut down the bank here to a stile which leads to a road.

(14) Go right and follow the road as it bends left to Ravensclough Farm. Just before the entrance to the farm, cross a stile on the right and head across the small enclosure to another stile which leads into Ravensclough wood, a woodland most aptly named. The path hugs the left-hand bank of the clough down to the flooding pastures of the River Dane. Your way is ahead across the meadow to climb up the small bank ahead. The path then curves left and right parallel with a tributary stream to your left. The path crosses a stone bridge and continues ahead to the embankment of the old railway, the meeting point with The Gritstone Trail. Cross the stile, climb the embankment and go right along the old trackbed for half a mile to the old Rushton railway station and The Knot Inn, a good place to take a spot of refreshment.

RUSHTON SPENCER TO CHEDDLETON

Route: Rushton Spencer – Ryecroft Gate – Rudyard – Longsdon – Deep Hayes – Cheddleton

Distance: 10 miles

Map: O.S. Pathfinder Map 792 Kidsgrove and Leek

Start: The Knot Inn, Rushton Spencer

Access: Rushton is served by the daily GM buses 201 service between Manchester and Derby via Leek. Car drivers should travel on the A523 between Leek and Macclesfield.

Rushton Spencer

For the walker, Rushton Spencer must be one of the finest areas of Staffordshire to explore. The Gritstone Trail leads off into Cheshire's high hills, towards Tegg's Nose Country Park, and The Staffordshire Way takes you to the charm of Rudyard Lake. There are also dozens of local walks through exceptional countryside such as up the Dane Valley to Wincle and Gradbach, although these paths are far more popular now. Other routes are less busy but still offer interesting walking such as to The Cloud, Lask Edge or through the quiet lanes in and around Heaton and Gun Hill. There are also four surviving public houses to quench the ramblers thirst afterwards.

One of the loveliest churches for miles around, St Lawrence stands apart from the village which it serves. Nestled on a hillside above the valley with its wooden bellcote and solid stone walls the church has an erstwhile appeal which is not found elsewhere, hence the description sometimes quoted "Chapel in the Wilderness". Inside, it still reflects its medieval origins.

Rushton Spencer from the churchyard of St Lawrence

Rudyard

A travel guide written in 1908 describes Rudyard as "one of the best known holiday resorts in North Staffordshire". By the turn of the century Rudyard certainly was the premier local destination for people escaping the grime of Potteries life at that time. The North Staffordshire Railway, who published the guide, was responsible for opening up Rudyard to excursionists and during the early decades ran special trains along the route at holiday times. There are instances cited when thousands turned up by trains to see major events such as the swimming of the Lake by Captain Webb in the summer of 1877.

Despite changing fortunes, not least the demise of the railway, Rudyard retains a haunting charm which attracts the would be walker to its tranquil shores. It retains the sort of appeal that prompted a young Potteries couple to name their son after this favourite location: "Rudyard" Kipling. Kipling, born in India, rarely returned to North Staffordshire but the association has not been forgotten and his works are read throughout the world.

Rudyard Lake

Leek

While not on the route, many walkers will divert to the town that now calls itself "The Queen of The Moorlands" reflecting a campaign to improve the physical and social fabric of the central part of town. Like so many small industrial cum market towns in mid England Leek has suffered through the loss of traditional manufacturing and an erosion of high street shopping facilities at the hand of larger centres and supermarkets.

What Leek has managed to do is retain a pride and a real character that has long since gone in other towns. Its silk and textile heritage is reflected in the fine mill buildings that have survived. Many of these now are antiques centres, restoring and selling furniture for the USA and UK markets. There are old quarters which beckon the visitor. The impressive church of St Edward the Confessor, the ornate Victorian Nicholson Institute, the marketplace thronging with stalls on a Wednesday all make Leek a pleasant place to stay awhile.

Leek is also a good access point for miles of walking through to Tittesworth, into the Churnet valley, to Waterhouse and The Manifold and so on. Having lost its station years ago the town still enjoys a good network of local buses so exploring Moorland villages and nearby towns is still a plausible option without a car. Except for the Roaches, which is a honeypot area for ramblers and climbers, most of the paths and by ways of the Moorlands are relatively quiet.

Deep Hayes Country Park

Originally a top-up reservoir to feed water into the River Churnet until the late 1970s, the area has now become an established country park. The valley in which the park is situated was once a small industrial zone with small scale coal mining and iron smelting as well as the digging of clay for the making of bricks. It is now a tranquil valley trodden only by recreationalists.

Refreshment and Accommodation:

Refreshment and accommodation are available in Rushton and Rudyard as well as Leek.

The Route

(1) The Staffordshire Way runs between the splendidly restored old station (a private residence complete with platforms in the garden!) and Knot Inn towards Rudyard Lake. This section is straightforward as the route follows the old trackbed of the original North Staffordshire Railway. The path crosses a road near Ryecroft Gate, a small settlement outside Rushton.

(2) Walk ahead alongside a dusty track where cars access to the northern shores of the reservoir. Go right before the lake over a small bridge. At the far end of the lake turn left along a track. The track bears right away from the shore and then forks within a few hundred metres. Take the left-hand fork which passes Cliffe Park.

(3) Continue ahead along the track in woodland, by the sailing club. After half a mile the track bears right and begins to climb. However, look for a signposted path on the left that passes through scrub then beneath a chalet bungalow to join another track through woodland. This curves right and climbs up between houses with a caravan site to the left. Cut left on a narrower path through to another track that runs behind houses to a road in Rudyard, a road which used to become very congested with visitors cars before restrictions were enforced. Look for a link path on the left by a house and before the car park of Hotel Rudyard. This drops down to the lakeside.

(4) The path drops to the right of the dam and alongside the conduit to the road. The Poacher public house is to the right, a few strides up the bank. Otherwise, continue ahead by an area of wet ground that is a haven for wildlife. The path bends to the left to run beneath a wood.

(5) It then follows the conduit through a valley for nearly two miles to the main A road on the outskirts of Leek. Turn right and after a few paces go right down a track by the Highway depot. Cross a stile to enter a field behind houses. Follow the path left near to the fence. Mid-way, cut slightly right to a stile by a gate in the upper boundary.

The path bears left through the wood, crosses a stile, then climbs up to another stile. Cross this and keep company with the fence on the

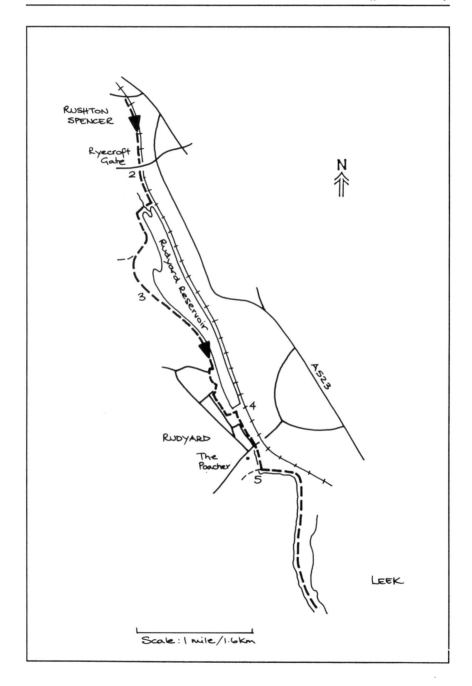

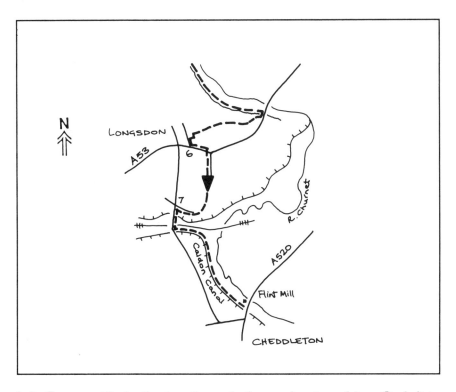

left. Cross a stile in the top through the garden to a drive. Go left to reach a road and turn left again to the main road.

(6) Bear left to walk back towards Leek. Before the corner cross the main road with care to go down Mollatts Wood Road. The road gives out to a track by a wall then a fence. This leads to a drive. Ahead is an electricity pole. Make your way down a track to the right of this to walk through hamlet known as Horse Bridge, another reminder of canal days.

(7) The track soon joins a road. Turn left and walk down to pass over the Leek branch of the Caldon Canal and, at the Caldon itself, go left to join the towpath. Follow this through the Churnet valley to Cheddleton entering the village by the Flint Mill. A track leads from the canal to the main road. Turn right for the main shops and old village quarter.

CHEDDLETON TO ALTON

Route: Cheddleton – Consall Forge – Kingsley – Kingsley Holt –
Hawksmoor – Dimmingsdale – Alton

Distance: 11 miles

Map: O.S. Pathfinders 792 Kidsgrove and Leek and 810 Ashbourne
and Churnet Valley

Start: Cheddleton Flint Mill

Access: Cheddleton is well served by bus from Hanley, Leek and
Longton including an hourly Sunday service on the Leek to Hanley
route. Telephone Staffordshire Busline on (0785) 223344 for details.
Cheddleton is on the main A520 road between Meir and Leek. There
is limited car parking in lay-bys at the top (southern) end of the
village.

Cheddleton

Cheddleton is a large village that has both dormitory housing and a
local industrial estate on what was the old Brittains paper mill. By far
the most interesting feature of the village is the Flint Mill sitting
between the Churnet river and the Caldon canal. Unusually, it has
two surviving water-wheels that were used to power the grinding of
flints brought from the South East of England by canal. The resulting
powder was used by pottery manufacturers to whiten and strengthen
china. The mill site is open at reasonable hours and on occasion the
machinery is set to use, a magnificent Heath Robinson type of affair
which fascinates even those not mechanically minded.

From the mill, the imposing church of St Edward the Confessor can
be seen. William Morris, philosopher and planner, is said to have
been involved in restoration on the church during the last century
and many of the stained glass windows are his work. Near to the
church are stone cottages, a pound and stocks. There are many
pleasant walks in and around the village from this quarter.

The Flint Mill, Cheddleton

Consall Forge

Despite the name, the area looks as if the fingers of industrialisation had not touched this secluded spot. The kilns alongside the canal tell a different story for the area was an important industrial pocket in earlier times with iron production as well as quarrying, the materials being transported on the navigation. Evidence suggests that there has been iron working in the valley since medieval times but it was not until the eighteenth century that the scale of the activity increased substantially.

Nearby is Consall Nature Park, opened in 1989 to the public but as its name suggests, the emphasis is more on nature conservation than opening up the surrounding areas. There is a visitor centre and a number of walks waymarked from here into the surrounding countryside.

Opposite: Pottery at Consall Forge

Kingsley

The same could be said of Kingsley which, for centuries, engaged in mining, quarrying, smelting and forging. Much of the industry moved to Froghall, the terminus of the Caldon Canal, where Bolton's cable works eventually settled. The medieval tower of Kingsley church guides the rambler across the fields to the village. The churchyard is a fascinating source of social history with a number of very old gravestones still surviving.

Accommodation and Refreshment:

Bed and Breakfast is available in the village of Cheddleton as are camping and caravanning at the Glencote Caravan site. Contact the Tourist Information Centre at Leek on (0538) 381000.

The Black Lion (two minutes from the Red Lion by Cheddleton parish church), Red Lion (on the A520 road) and The Boat public houses serve refreshment. The refreshment rooms at the North Staffordshire Railway Centre are often open during afternoons in summer and at weekends throughout the year. There are shops on the main road.

The Staffordshire Way passes one of Staffordshire's more famous pubs, The Black Lion at Consall Forge, which usually opens at lunch-time as well as evenings. There are pubs at Kingsley, a one minute diversion from the Way at Kingsley church. There are also public houses in Kingsley Holt, near the church. The cafe-cum-restaurant known as The Ramblers Retreat, a mile before Alton, is a popular refreshment stop. It is usually open at lunchtimes as well as evenings.

The Route

(1) Start from the Flint Mill in Cheddleton. Retrace your steps to the towpath and turn left to walk under the road and then by locks down to the first bridge where The Boat Inn is to the right and The North Staffordshire Railway to the left.

(2) The route follows the towpath of the Caldon Canal through the Churnet Valley, wide at first but narrowing as it approaches Consall Forge. This 2 mile section offers a tranquil sojourn from life. Herons take flight at the slightest noise and blue kingfishers can be seen darting above the Churnet. Boats are often moored at Bridge 47 and not far beyond is a traditional drawbridge of which there are few on this canal. At Lock 16, the canal and river combine until Consall Forge and your path now crosses to the other side. The towpath passes through wet ground and by old lime kilns at Coal-pit Wood and Consall Forge just over half a mile away. You will also pass two milestones standing side by side. The earliest dates from a time when the canal terminated at Froghall (as it does now) and is over 200 years old.

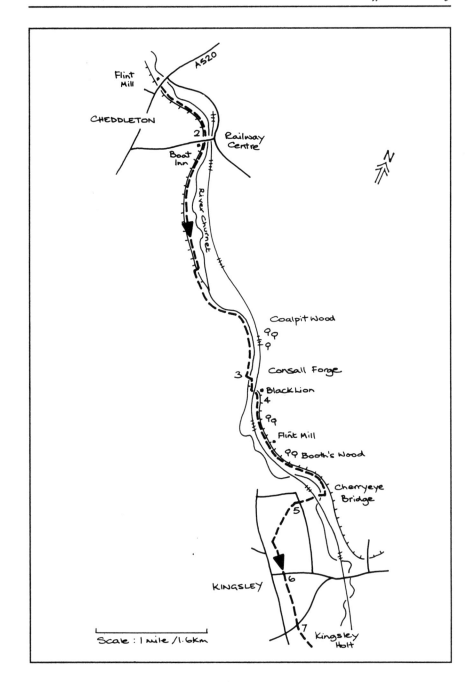

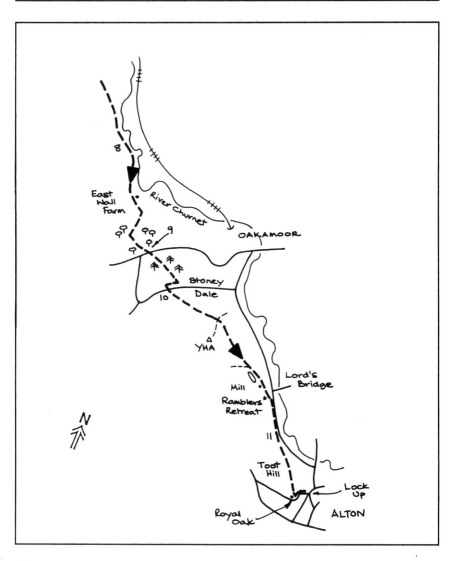

(3) You need to cross the footbridge and the stone canal bridge. Temptation certainly stands in your way here, for the Black Lion on the left is a compulsory stop for the weary rambler. For the strong willed, your way is under the railway, which then happens to be squeezed between the canal and river along the next section. The small platform shelter seen on the right at Consall Forge halt is

maintained by a group of enthusiasts who worship the day when a steam hauled passenger service is restored. An early guide described the route as one of the most picturesque lines in England and many curse the day when British Rail closed it to passenger traffic in the 1960s. Not all feel so enthusiastic about the re-emergence of passenger railway here, for they are concerned about the impact of a steam railway on the more sensitive environments in and around Consall Nature reserve.

Perhaps part of the track could be converted to an off-road cycle route?

(4) The route then follows the canal to the old Consall flint mill passing by a small pottery en route. The path then dips beneath Booth's Wood where the smell of wild garlic pervades the valley in springtime. The towpath comes to Cherryeye Bridge, a tight bridge for navigators and then 300 metres beyond look for a stile on the right. The path crosses the river and then sweeps under the railway then very shortly rising to the right through wet ground to a stile that exits onto Banks Lane. Take a deep breath, for there's more climbing to come.

(5) Cross the road and then climb steps up the steep hillside with a falconry to the right. The path reaches a stile at the top of the wood. It then continues ahead to a stile in the next boundary and through another field in a similar direction to a gap stile by a barred gate. Go through this and head slightly left to the top far left corner. Go over the steps and stile and walk ahead to a gate before a farm. Do not go through but instead cut right through a kissing gate into the church-yard.

Those diverting into Kingsley should follow a path around the right of the church. Otherwise, bear left to pass to the left of the church and exit by a kissing gate onto a lane. Continue ahead to the main Dovedale Road.

(6) Cross the road and pass to the right of the Kingsley War Memorial. Cross the stile by the signpost to Hawksmoor. Cross a stile by a gateway, then bear left down to another stile. Head slightly right over the next field and cross a stile nearer to the houses and

slightly right over the brow of the field. Cross a stile in the opposite boundary and follow the path as it curves right with the raised hedge and fencing. Cross a stile by the fence and proceed slightly right across the field towards the small church at Kingsley Holt. Before reaching it turn left along a track between houses to the main road.

(7) Cross the road and walk a few paces to the right before going left over a stile into fields again, fields which lead down to one of the most beautiful sections of The Way, above the banks of the Churnet. Walk ahead through the first pasture to cross a stile. Then, head slightly right down the next field to a stile and footbridge. Once over, head slightly left to drop down to a stile set in tree roots. Continue ahead through a gap in a straggling hedge and descend through hummocks to a footbridge over a stream. The path curves left and right through gorse and bushes to cross a stile, the Churnet winding below. You descend to an area of wet ground.

(8) Cross a stile over a tributary stream and follow the path as it rises over the bank and through a meadow to a stile by a National Trust sign. The path proceeds ahead towards East Wall Farm, a clearly defined route through low lying pastures. As you approach the farm head for a stile to the right of the out buildings and left of a pool. The path leads up to a track where you turn left and then follow it as it climbs through into the wood to a junction. Bear right here for a steeper climb up to the main road.

(9) Turn left and cross before the corner to turn right up a track into Sutton's Wood. The track winds to the right (i.e. avoid the left-hand fork) and then bends left to drop down between coniferous woods to a road. Turn right for a climb up Stoney Dale and then at the brow go left, as signposted to Dimmingsdale Youth Hostel. To the right of the track is a view across to Oldfurnace, a name which reflects early wood burning in the area.

(10) The track comes to a crossroads and those staying at the youth hostel turn right. Otherwise continue ahead down Ousal Dale to meet another well-walked route down Dimmingsdale at Earl's Rock. The path passes a pool and restored building, once a smelting mill to the unusually shaped Ramblers Retreat, serving refreshment to all comers. The path curves to the right of the front of the building and

begins to climb above a car park. It joins another track and continues straight on to descend to the road again at a sharp corner.

(11) Your way is up the hill to Toothill Rocks, a scramble up a steep hillside (which can be avoided by walking along the road to Alton). The path gains height until it reaches the rocks and just beyond are stiles leading into a field. Bear slightly left up to a stile leading into a walled track. Go right and then first left. This drops down into Alton, exiting conveniently by the Royal Oak public house. Deviate from the route here to walk ahead up to Alton Lock Up and the main street. Turn left and then next right into High Street where the The Bull's Head, The White Hart and a cafe are available.

ALTON TO UTTOXETER

Route: Alton – Saltersford Lane – Denstone – Quixhill Bridge – Rocester – Eaton Hall Farm – Doveridge – Uttoxeter

Distance 8 miles

Map: O.S. Pathfinder maps 810 Ashbourne and The Churnet Valley and 851 Uttoxeter

Access: Alton is served by buses from Hanley (although sometimes there is a change required at Cheadle) and Uttoxeter. Rocester is served by buses from Cheadle, Ashbourne and Uttoxeter. There are no Sunday buses. Contact Staffordshire Busline for details on (0785) 223344

Accommodation and Refreshment:

Alton has several guest houses. It can get very busy in the height of Summer when people are visiting nearby Alton Towers. There is also guest house accommodation in the Rocester area but less than Alton. Uttoxeter has both small hotels and guest houses. There are pubs, shops and a cafe in Alton. Denstone has a pub and shop and Rocester has several so it is a well-watered stretch of the walk.

Alton

The setting of Alton village on the craggy edge of the incised Churnet valley is quite dramatic. In particular the haunting Gothic castle gives an impression that this is fanciful fortress might well be on the Rhine. Designed by Pugin and financed by the 16th Earl of Shrewsbury this mock structure stands near to scant ruins of a medieval castle. It was built as a resting place for priests in later life but then became a convent.

The Way enters the village by a different route, so it might be worth walking down into the valley perhaps to the old railway station, also designed by Pugin, where there is a

Alton Castle

is a good view. The entire area became known as "The Little Switzerland" of Staffordshire.

Across the valley stands one of England's most popular theme parks, Alton Towers. Set in parkland created for the Earls of Shrewsbury, this has to be one of the most pleasant sites for a theme park, matching any in continental Europe for scenic beauty, a modern day version of Beauty and the Beast (for the uninitiated the latter is a ride).

The village itself suffers from coaches passing through, but stands up remarkably well to the Summertime movement. There are many endearing features such as the lock up, a honeycombed round building that was used at one time to incarcerate villains.

Denstone

The village is best known for its college sponsored by Sir Thomas Percival Heywood and founded by Nathanial Woodward, a great school builder of the last century. He also took pride in seeing to the restoration of the nearby church, a very Gothic looking structure designed by Street. The village was well known earlier in the century for its damsons some of which were despatched to local markets and other to the dye works of Lancashire. Damsons are still grown in and around the village.

Rocester

Lying on slightly higher ground between the waters of the Churnet and Dove, the village of Rocester has been a fording point across the valley since Roman times. The site of a Roman fortress has been identified but there are no tangible remains of their occupation of this community, despite the name. To many, the village is something of a disappoint-

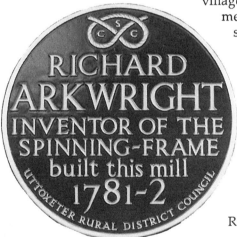

ment with modern housing and shops dominating the central core. The landscape to the west is now dominated by J.C Bamford, the maker of diggers, tractors and other equipment that is revered by farmers throughout the world. On the eastern side of the village the Way passes by Rocester church, and then the Tutbury Mill, said to have been built by Richard Arkwright in 1782.

The Route

(1) From wherever you are staying in Alton, make your way to Town Head along the end of High Street or, if following the official route, by St Peters church. At the end of High Street bear right into Hurstons Lane and look for a stile on the left into a field. Head slightly left to the next stile and then ahead in the following enclosure to a stile that leads into Saltersford Lane, a rather wet green lane at the best of times. Fortunately, there are slabs down on one side and farther along these become real gritstone slabs that seem more appropriate for such a historic route.

(2) The lane continues for almost a mile before opening up at a stile. Keep company with the hedge on the right to cross a stile and then follow the field's edge on the right again as it bends right. Then, cut across the field towards the wooded bluff where another stile is crossed. The path then tapers to a stream. Cross the footbridge and stile and walk ahead towards Denstone church until a road is reached. Cross the road and turn left to walk down the hill to the Quixhill Bridge.

(3) Once over the bridge go right over a stile, the signposted marking the path to Rocester. On the opposite side of the road are ornate stone gates leading to the JCB testing area which happens to be private. Head for a stile just to the right of two large solitary trees in the next boundary. Cross it and make your way ahead to a double stile guarding a bridge.

(4) Cross here and make your way along the river for a few paces before going up the bank to a stile into a wood. Cross it and go right to climb gently again, but with a dip for a stream before the last push up to a stile leading into a field. Cross it and walk a few paces up the bank to a signpost, then bear slightly right to descend the field. The JCB factory can be seen ahead and Rocester to the left. The former is best seen at dusk when the lights reflect in the gentle ripple of the water.

(5) Use your ingenuity to cross the by pass and then turn next left to walk along a road into Rocester, planted with trees but no path for

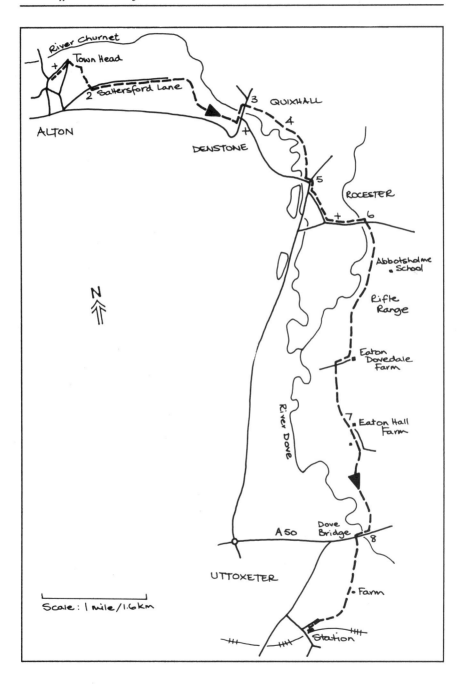

walkers as yet. At the main junction in the village turn left to walk by
the flats. The road passes by the church and then Tutbury Mill to the
bridge over the River Dove.

(6) Go down the steps to the riverside fields along the Dove. Walk
ahead to cross a footbridge and progress in a similar direction to
cross a stile by a gate. Abbotsholme school stands to the left up the
hillside. The river meanders to the right but you cross a stile (the one
on the left) into playing fields. Turn left to follow a hedge by a brook
and go to a footbridge. Cross it and turn right to walk beneath trees
then along the river's edge before turning left along a green path to a
line of willow trees, keeping to the right of a ditch. Cross a stile by a
gate and continue straight on to cross another stile by a gate. Join a
track. Approach a farm but go right down a track and then after the
first field turn left as signposted to Doveridge.

(7) The main track goes right before Eaton Hall Farm but you go
through a barred gate, passing to the right of buildings. The gate is
awkward and the track often gets muddy. Go through the next gate
then turn right to pass through the shooting club. Go through a
gateway at the top of the bank and turn right along the field's edge.
This runs along the edge of a wood to a stile. Once across, go left and
at the signpost bear right. This follows the edge at first but then
drops down to a stile between hawthorns by a stream.

(8) Head for the Dove Bridge. There is a stile in the fence to the left
of the old bridge. Go through it and turn right to cross the bridge,
then go down and up steps to join the main road. Cross the road
with extreme care and turn right along for about 200 metres. Turn
left to enter fields and walk diagonally across the field heading for
the electricity pylons. Keep in a similar direction across wet ground
to a stile in a fence on the right. Cross this and then turn left to cross
another stile. Approach the farm but turn right to walk along a lane
by it but only to cross a stile on the left into a field again. Head
diagonally right to the corner where another stile is crossed. Go
ahead towards the railway with a view of the race-course on the left.
Reach rough ground where railway tracks once existed. The Way is
unclear here and beware of development that might alter the route.
Your way is slightly right along a main track to a gate. This exits
onto a road by the works. Uttoxter railway station is on the left.

UTTOXETER TO ABBOTS BROMLEY

Route: Uttoxeter Railway Station- Timber Lane – Knightslands Farm – Marlpit House Farm – Bagot's Park – Abbots Bromley

Distance: 7 miles

Maps: O.S. Pathfinder maps 831 Uttoxeter and 851 Abbots Bromley

Start: Uttoxeter Railway Station

Access: Uttoxeter is well served by train (daily service) and bus. Abbots Bromley is connected by bus from Uttoxeter and Stafford but these tend to be a school times or market day. Thus, it is more difficult to plan a day walk on this section using local buses but not impossible. The authors suggest that you might like to extend to a day's rambling to Colwich where there is a regular daily bus service to Stafford.

Uttoxeter

The narrow streets of Uttoxeter leading away from the marketplace make the town an interesting place to visit on foot for there are several nooks and crannies where old buildings still stand. There is also a monument dedicated to Dr Johnson in the centre. This marks the spot where he stood bare-headed in the rain at the age of 70 as a penance for not helping on his father's book-stall at a considerably younger age. Just around the corner is the Uttoxeter Heritage Centre, in restored 17th century half-timbered cot-

Accommodation and Refreshment:

Uttoxeter and Abbots Bromley offer accommodation and have several public houses serving refreshment.

tages. The centre illustrates the way of life hereabouts in previous centuries.

Uttoxeter swells with people on a market day when people come in from villages and farms. Otherwise, like so many small English towns, it tends to be very quiet and the number of shops for sale lends credence to the argument that the local economy is depressed. The parish church is an impressive landmark in the town and there are several good-looking Georgian town houses in this quarter, spoiled only by a sprawling car park.

Winter walking at Bagot's Wood

The Walk

(1) From Uttoxeter Railway Station walk along Brookside Road. As the road bends right towards town, there are steps up to the main road on the left. Cross the main road and turn left over the bridge. The sidings on the right have all gone. All that remains is a distinctive railway building which is falling into a poor state of repair, as are many old buildings along the lineside in Uttoxeter. If only a suitable use could be found. Just after the former entrance to the sidings, go right through a kissing gate and proceed across the field to houses.

(2) Walk along Bank Close and turn left into Balance Hill, a name that reflects the importance of sheep farming in the area, when fleeces would be weighed on a balance. Turn almost immediately right into West Hill, signposted as a "No Through Road". As this bears sharp right you continue ahead along a hedged track. Cross the road through a recent housing estate and proceed along the track to go through a gate, where a caravan stands to the right.

(3) A good 100 metres before Field Head Farm leave the track to head slightly right by an electricity pole to a stile to the right of the farm buildings. Cross it and head in a similar direction up the next field to cross a stile into Timber Lane, a green lane. Follow this to a road.

(4) Go over the road and follow a path to the left of a drive to Knightsfield Farm. Cross the tracks to the left of the barn then walk straight on to a stile. Once over, your way is along the hedge which is now to your left. The path dips down to a little stream and up to another stile. Cross this and keep ahead again but ensure that you are to the right of an electricity pole. Cross a stile by a pool on you right and walk on through two more level fields. Approach Knights-lands Farm, to your right. The path crosses a footbridge and joins a track.

(5) Go left and immediately right to cross a stile. Aim for the far left corner where you exit onto a road. Turn right and after 200 metres

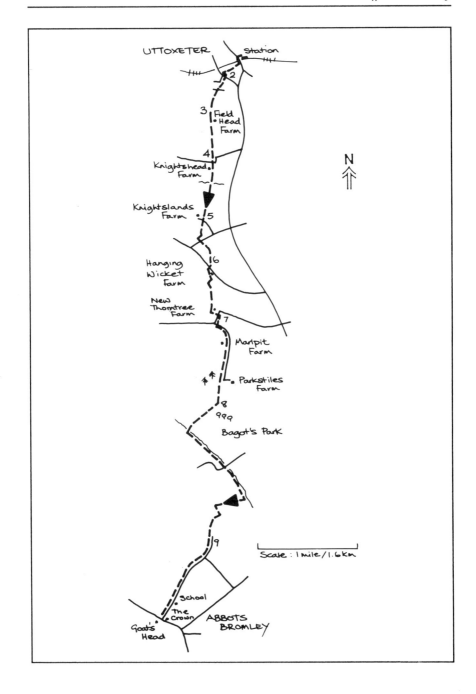

cross a stile on the left. Keep company with the hedge on your right and cross fencing mid-way along it into an adjacent field. Head diagonally left across the field to emerge onto a road.

(6) Turn left and after a few paces right over a stile into low lying pastures again. Walk along the edge of a paddock and cross a stile. Hanging Wicket Farm stands to your left. Then proceed slightly right up a field towards a stile which sits to the right of a group of ash trees. Cross it and turn right to the field corner where you bear left to follow the field's edge. This leads to stiles guarding a footbridge. Once over walk onward to the next field corner to cross a stile, then bear left along a track. Do not be tempted to follow it! Before the barred gate go right over a stile by a tree and walk the field with New Thorntree Farm on the left, no doubt standing on the site of an old Thorntree Farm. Cross a stile by a gate and ahead to cross another onto a road.

(7) Go right and at the junction bear left to Marlpit Farm. Walk through the farmyard between farm buildings and the farmhouse on the left. The track proceeds to a gate and junction. Keep ahead here but as the road bends left, go ahead on a green lane along the edge of Hill's Wood. Parkstiles Farm stands to your left. You soon reach a signpost where you enter a large field in Bagot's Park. Bear slightly right to a brow in the field and then head for the right end of a line of trees. The path bends right just before to cross a stile by a gate.

(8) Join a track and turn right along it. The track descends to cross Story Brook. Go left to walk down the field. Go over a farm access road and continue alongside the brook through another large field. At the corner it bends right to climb up through a small wood and ahead to a stile that allows you to cross the hedge. Once over turn right to follow the field boundary to the right and then back down left to a gateway. Go right here and keep company with a hedge on your right. Follow this until you reach a stile and signpost allowing you to cross the boundary again. Turn left and now follow the hedge on your left to cross another stile by a gate. The path climbs up to a track, known as Hobfield Lane, and shortly a road.

(9) Walk along the road to enter the outskirts of Abbots Bromley by an old school and schoolhouse. Walk down School Lane to the village centre where the Butter Cross sits neatly between two ancient hostelries, The Goat and The Crown.

Nearing Abbots Bromley

ABBOTS BROMLEY TO GREAT HAYWOOD

Route: Abbots Bromley – Stockwell Heath – Colton – Trent and Mersey Canal – Great Hayward

Distance: 9 miles

Map: O.S. Pathfinder sheets 851 Abbots Bromley and 850 Stafford

Start: The Butter Cross, Abbots Bromley

Access: Abbots Bromley is not well-served by bus. There is a sporadic service from Uttoxeter. By car it is possible to travel on the B5013 from Uttoxter or Rugeley. There is limited on-street parking in Abbots Bromley.

Abbots Bromley

Abbots Bromley is famous for its annual Horn Dance. This is re-enacted on the first Monday after the 4th September. Six men wearing costume and ancient reindeer antlers dance their way through the parish for most of the day, a gruelling experience requiring considerable stamina and the ability to consume large volumes of liquid refreshment at the various stopping places. They should also preferably not be camera-shy, for hundreds turn up to photograph the event. The antlers, some of which have been dated from the 11th century, can be seen in Abbots Bromley church at other times.

Should you not happen to be passing on the said date in September, Abbots Bromley still holds much in store for the visitor. The architecture is delightful, being a mixture of Georgian and Victorian townhouses, half-timbered cottages and to crown it all, a hexagonal timber Butter Cross. This is undeniably the centre of the village, no doubt where coaches drew up in the coaching days before the arrival of railways. The railway, however, never came to Abbots Bromley and only buses stop here now. Two inns, which date from coaching times, face each other across what is almost a little square and there's a busy feel about the place. People call into the village shop or for petrol at the garage which has not changed much in recent times. There must be heritage value in old petrol pumps.

The church is situated in a quiet backwater a stone's throw away from the Butter Cross, a medieval structure restored in the last century but retaining brasses and monuments from earlier centuries as well as the Horn Dance antlers. It is well worth a visit.

The traditional Horn Dance

Colton

The Way passes through one end of Colton, with houses reaching its picturesque church that happened to be restored by Street, the same ecclesiastical architect who worked at Abbots Bromley in the last century. Colton also contains several distinctive houses such as the Queen Anne Colton House, said to stand on the site of an earlier manor. On leaving the village, you cross the appropriately named Brook Bridge, which includes four large boulders deposited hereabouts during glacial times.

The ford and bridge at Colton

Colwich

Transport has dominated the fate of this village with two main roads running through, a railway junction and the Trent and Mersey Canal alongside the River Trent itself. The canal was built to bring raw materials into The Potteries and transport finished goods to other parts of the country. Known as The Grand Trunk the navigation was originally engineered by James Brindley before his death. The handsome church seen from the canal is mainly Victorian containing several monuments to the Wolseley family of the former Wolseley Hall and also belonging to the Anson family of Shugborough.

The Walk

(1) From the Butter Cross, facing the Goats Head Inn, turn left and then right at the junction to the church. Pass to the right of the church to a kissing gate in the far corner of the churchyard. Walk along the metalled footpath but look for a stile on the left entering a field. Walk ahead, parallel with the stream to a bridge that has seen better days. Cross the stile onto a lane.

(2) Turn right and just beyond the sewerage works as the lane curves to the right, go ahead through a gap by a barred gate. Follow the field hedge around to the left to cross a stile onto a road. Go right and within one hundred paces cross a stile on the left. Walk up the field to cross another stile and then onward to join a narrow green track. This meets another wider green lane. You go left here to join a road. There are glimpses of Blithfield Reservoir here. You will not see much more than the dam for the next two miles.

(3) Turn right to walk towards the building but beforehand cut left and then almost immediately right between poles (another quaint Abbots Bromley custom?) to a stile. Go over it and walk ahead to join a track bearing left through a gate. The track crosses the River Blithe full with fresh, sparkling waters from the Blithfield Reservoir to your right. Once over the bridge go left along the river bank, but as the river meanders left, turn right over a footbridge, and to a stile in a hedge. Cross it and walk ahead along the field's edge. Cross a stile and turn right along a lane.

Refreshment and Accommodation:

Abbots Bromley has a shop opposite the Butter Cross and several inns including the Goats Head, The Crown and The Royal Oak. All three offer food. Accommodation is available in the village.

The Way also passes through Colton and Colwich both of which have a shop and pub.

(4) Follow this until you reach a signpost. Cross the stile here to enter a field and bear right up the field to another signpost. Turn left and proceed through a very muddy section to Medleywood Barn, probably

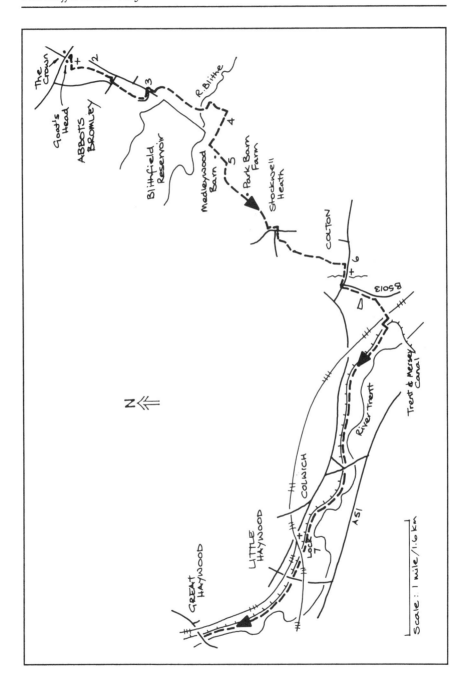

the worst section of the route. The path crosses a stile by the barn. Keep ahead and towards the end of the field cross a stiles by a gate. The ground underfoot becomes easier going. Cross a double stile and footbridge over a ditch known as Park Pale, an ancient boundary.

(5) The path continues ahead through fields, behind Park Barn Farm, and onto a track. Follow this ahead to a metalled road at Stockwell Heath. Turn left and right by the pool. The road passes a house as it bends to the left. Just past cottages cross a stile on the left and another within a few paces. Go straight on to a double stile and footbridge. Then, bear right across the next enclosure to cross a stile and then ahead to walk through a small enclosure and a stile. Keep ahead now through three more stiles by gates. After the latter go slightly right over the field, cross another stile and maintain a similar direction. Cross a stile into a paddock and go over a stile in the hedge. Go right and walk towards Colton Village Hall. The Way passes in front of the building and along a track to a road.

(6) Go right along the pavement to a bridge and ford with a good view across to the little church at Colton, standing serenely near the brook. You come to a junction with the B5013. Cross the road and turn left to follow the pavement by a lodge and Boathouse Spinney. The road bends left and you turn right down a track through fields to cross the railway. Turn right down to the towpath and walk ahead to Colwich lock. There's a cut off point here by crossing the towpath by the lock keeper's house and ahead to the church where buses for Stafford depart at least hourly and often half-hourly intervals.

(7) Otherwise, continue along the towpath to Great Haywood where you leave the Trent and Mersey at Bridge 73. Turn right for the village shops and inns. Go left if continuing on the route.

GREAT HAYWOOD TO PENKRIDGE

Route: Great Haywood – Shugborough – The Punch Bowl – Bednall – Teddesley Park – Penkridge

Distance: 6 miles

Map: O.S. Pathfinder 850 Stafford and 871 Cannock North

Start: The Essex Bridge, Great Haywood

Access: Great Haywood is served by a regular daily bus service from Stafford. The village is just off the A51 road and there is a limited amount of on street parking.

Shugborough

There is no better way to approach Shugborough than on foot across the beautifully arched Essex Bridge spanning the River Trent just below its confluence with the Sow. Shugborough Hall and parkland must be one of the glories of the county. The hall was built in the mid 1690s but much improved during the 18th century by Thomas Anson, an eccentric and self confessed dilettante, being a member of the Society of Dilettante! He enlisted the support of fellow member "Athenian" Stuart who was responsible for the obsessive classical structures erected throughout the parkland such as the Triumphal Arch seen from the route. Stuart created many of these features after spending time in Greece observing the dimensions and stiles of famous Greek monuments. In many respects he began a Neo-Greek architectural movement in Britain and Shugborough is one of the earliest projects. You pass near to The Tower of Winds, for example, which is a reproduction of the Horlogium of Andronikos Cyrrhestes in Athens.

Thomas, George Anson's older brother, established a reputation as an exceptional Admiral in the British navy during the early part of the 18th century. Following his death in 1762, Thomas spent the remainder of his life and much of their combined wealth in setting out the estate much as we see it today, partly as a tribute to the brother he so admired. Shugborough is now home to the 5th Earl of Lichfield, the incumbent being better known as Patrick Lichfield, a famous photographer.

The Mansion House, Park Farm and gardens are open to the public.

Cannock Chase

The ancient Royal Forest of Cannock only looks ancient in certain places these days, for it is planted mainly with fast-growing coniferous soft woods. The Staffordshire Way skirts one of the oldest parts of the wood, Brocton Coppice, which is rich in oak and wildlife. Fallow deer still roam throughout and are not too perturbed by the passing walker. Perhaps, less well known is that Cannock Chase contains acres of heathland which encourages rich insect and birdlife.

The Way rises to a glacial boulder on which the Brocton Army camp water tower once stood. This was one of several large army camps situated in and around the Chase. As an amenity the Chase is much loved by local people offering dozens of opportunities for casual walking and sometimes cycling.

Bednall

Opposite: The Punch Bowl, Cannock Chase

The hamlet of Bednall is nestled around the Victorian church. It is typical of many small rural communities in that it has fought throughout recent decades to retain such basic facilities as the school and shop.

Accommodation and Refreshment:

There are shops and public houses in Great Haywood. Accommodation is available in Stafford.

The Staffordshire and Worcestershire Canal

The Staffordshire Way joins the Staffordshire and Worcestershire Canal on this section. This must surely be one of the loveliest canals in the county, perhaps more so farther south near to Kinver. Linking the Trent and Mersey with the Severn near Stourport, the canal hugs the contours, a characteristic of Brindley's approach to canal building particularly in the early years.

The Walk

(1) The Staffordshire Way leads triumphantly over the Essex Bridge into the grounds of Shugborough, along a straight metalled road with excellent views over parkland to the hall. The narrower fenced road meets a wider one by the home farm and continues ahead. As the access road bears right, you walk ahead to the main A513 road.

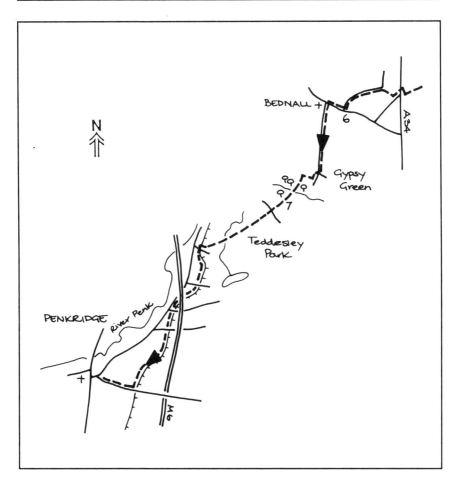

(2) Turn right to walk along the verge. It is not a particularly pleasant section but, as the road bends left, cross when traffic permits to join a wider verge. At the next corner as the road veers to the right walk straight on through the Punch Bowl Car Park. A well-worn route rises out of the parking area to an exceptional part of the Chase. The track descends to meet another at a major junction. Turn left here.

(3) Walk through the shade of the forest to a junction known as Stepping Stones, the said stones being to your left across the Sher Brook. Ignore them, however, for you stay on the main route ahead

through woodland, which gives out to heath. The path rises above the brook to a junction. Go right here and climb up the side of the valley to another junction. Go left at the main junction on the higher slopes of the hillside. Follow this along the hillside to pass by the trig point. Nearby you will see a glacial boulder on the site of the old Brocton Army Camp.

(4) Cross the Chase Road by the parking lay-bys. The way continues as a narrow path through scrub, crossing a green way, and down the Oldacre Valley by way of a path on the right through gorse and then heather. It then joins a main track in the valley to go left up the hillside. The track continues to the left to a junction of ways. Go left here but almost immediately turn right to follow the worn route to Camp Road.

(5) Cross the road and almost opposite is a gate. Follow the gap between swaying tall pine trees. Follow the track down to the A34 road. Go right and then cross over. Walk down Joyce's Lane. After the last house on the right cross a stile to enter a field, the first field encountered since Colton. Walk straight on to the field corner where you cross a stile. Keep company with the hedge on the left to a green lane. Go left down it towards Bednall.

(6) Turn right to walk down to the junction before Bednall church, signposted to Teddesley. Follow this metalled road, known as Cock Lane, to a junction with the access road to Gypsy Green. Not far beyond look for a stile on the right into fields. Walk to the top field corner. Cross a stile here and head slightly left towards the wood. Cross a stile into the woodland and keep ahead over a stream and to the parkland of Teddesley.

(7) Follow a fence to a road. Go over this and go straight on again down the hillside to a field corner by a stream. Head for the footbridge over a stream. Head slightly left towards the boatyard on the canal. Cross a stile by a gate and walk over the canal bridge onto the turn right onto the towpath. Go under the bridge and follow the canalside path for nearly two miles to Penkridge.

PENKRIDGE TO CODSALL

Route: Penkridge – Preston Vale – Mitton – Bickford Meadows – Lapley – Telford Aqueduct – Brewood – Gunstone Hall -Codsall

Distance: 13.5 miles

Map: O.S. Pathfinder Map 871 Cannock North and 891 Wolverhampton North

Start: Penkridge Parish Church

Access: There is a Mondays to Saturdays train service from Stafford and Wolverhampton. There is also a regular daily bus service.

Penkridge

The small town of Penkridge, south of Stafford, has been a stopping-off point for travellers since Roman times. Its wide thoroughfare still houses several substantial coaching inns, including the half-timbered White Hart, said to have accommodated Queen Elizabeth when journeying through Staffordshire. Amid an old quarter of Georgian and Victorian houses stands the inspiring church of Saint Michael and All Angels, a church that has many fine artefacts including tombs belonging to local landowning families the Wynnesburys and Littletons. Nearby is Penkridge market where a small amount of livestock trading still exists, also open stalls on Wednesday and Saturday.

Lapley

The Staffordshire Way brings the walker directly to Lapley church with its very large central tower. The church stands on the site of an earlier Benedictine monastery and this could well offer an explanation as to the larger than usual dimensions to this village church.

Nearby there are several distinctive houses, some of which have been tastefully restored in recent years in this out of the way settlement.

Sheep grazing in Churchyard, Lapley

Brewood

Like Lapley, Brewood is one of the prettiest villages (or small town) in South Staffordshire running from the marketplace down to the grand church. There are several unusual buildings in the main street including Speedwell Castle, an ornate Gothic town house dating from the mid 18th century evidently built on the winnings of a bet made on a horse named Speedwell!

Accommodation and Refreshment:

Penkridge offers accommodation, pubs and shops. There is limited accommodation at Wheaton Aston (near Lapley) and Brewood. All have public houses and Brewood has a variety of shops.

While the Shropshire Union canal did not bring industrialisation to Brewood it did bring trade. Wharves remain and there are a number of hostelries near to the navigation. The Shropshire must be one of the prettiest mainline canals to have been built. It was engineered by Telford, running from Autherley Junction in the West Midlands to Ellesmere Port in Cheshire. The building of the canal was problematic in Staffordshire with many cuttings and embankments, an engineer's dream – but a nightmare in terms of construction costs.

Speedwell Castle

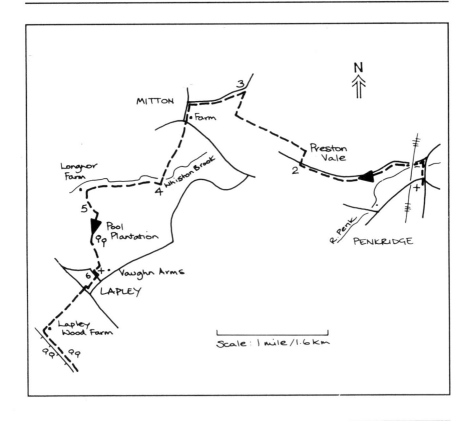

The Walk

(1) From the church in Penkridge, walk to the main A449 road and turn left. Pass the market car park and over the River Penk. Turn next left and walk under the railway bridge. As the road bends right, continue along a narrow lane to Preston Vale, about a mile further on. Preston Vale is no more than a few houses and a farm.

(2) Go right over a stile just beyond Perton Cottage, signposted to Mitton. Follow the field's edge to a corner and then left to continue along the far edge until the path meets a track. Go straight on until a jutting corner of a field where the path bears right and continues to a stile. Exit onto a road and turn left.

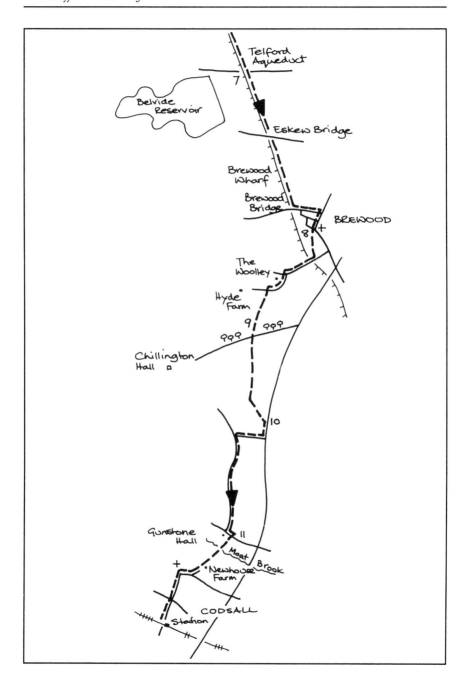

(3) This narrow lane comes to a junction. Go left and pass by Lower Mitton Farm. At the T junction go ahead on a bridleway, the second gateway to the left of the cottage. Go straight across the field to the corner of a pool and then cut right along a tractor track between crops to a gap. The path follows the field edge and drops down to a footbridge spanning the Whiston Brook to Bickford Meadows, a splendid conservation area amid large scale farming practice. The reserve belongs to The Staffordshire Wildlife Trust and they have erected information boards about the site.

(4) The path bends left and then right through the wet ground to a wicket gate. Go through it and walk ahead along a hedge to another wicket gate. Then go through a gap. The path curves around to the left to another gate and stile. Cross it and go right along the field's edge towards Longnor Farm. At the corner bear left to follow the hedge up the field towards Lapley, which can be seen in the near distance. At the large oak tree cut across the field to a double gate.

(5) Once through these, follow the field boundary on the left as it curves left to a corner. Cross the hedge here and turn right to keep company with a hedge on the right by Poll Plantation. Continue towards the church, going through a gateway and through a gap by a small pool. Keep ahead to pass by a house at the rear of the church (ignoring the stile on the right) to climb a small muddy embankment into the churchyard.

(6) Go left if refreshment is required at the Vaughan Arms. Otherwise, pass by the ancient church to a road. Go left and just before the hall turn right to enter a field as signposted. Follow the edge down to a section of old road by cottages. Turn right to join the new road. Cross here and walk down the track to Lapley Wood Farm. Go through the farmyard and then bear left at the canal bridge onto the Shropshire Union Canal. Walk beneath through delightful wooded cutting to Telford's Aqueduct just beyond the boatyard. To see it at its best you really have to divert down to the main road to view the ornate ironwork.

(7) Continue along the towpath, under Eskew Bridge and by Brewood Wharf to Brewood Bridge (No 14). Steps lead up to a road. Go right to pass the Bridge Inn and into the village centre where

there is a butcher and baker, chemist and grocery store, and several public houses. The road bends to the right by Speedwell Castle and passes by the church to another corner. Cross the road here and look for an alleyway on the right.

(8) This walled path soon joins a track. Turn left and then go first right over a stile into a field. A well-worn path leads down the field towards the canal. Cross two stiles before reaching another stile by an ivy clad footpath sign onto a canal bridge. Turn right along the track and pass by a house. The track comes to a junction. Turn left here, as signposted to Hyde Farm. The track soon bends right to skirt The Woolley and as it bends right to descend towards a stream go left over a stile into fields and follow a line of trees above rougher ground and woodland.

(9) You now approach the Avenue of Chillington Hall and Staffordshire Way waymarks become thicker on the ground, advising ramblers to keep to the path across the wide expanse of greenery leading up to the Hall itself to be seen in the distance to your right. Cross the road and ahead into a field once again. Cross a track and at the end of the next field cross a stile by a pool. A little path winds through a piece of woodland to a large field. Follow the field edge to the road.

(10) Turn right here and at the junction turn right again along a section of road through old workings. Turn first left down Gunstone Lane. This runs over the M54 motorway and up to Gunstone Farm. Shortly afterwards, you reach a junction at Gunstone Hall. Turn left and just beyond the entrance go over a stile into fields, often with horses running loose and sometimes wet under foot in Winter.

(11) The fencing on your right leads down to a bridge over Moat Brook. Once over, continue ahead two fields and stiles in a similar direction. Cross a stile before Newhouse Farm and one just to the right of it. Now, follow an access track ahead to a road. Go right and follow the road up to a corner by the church. It then bends left down the hill to cross Barkers Way. The bus stop on the right is for Wolverhampton. Walk through the shops, down Station road to Codsall Railway Station.

CODSALL TO SEISDON

Route: Codsall Railway Station – Oaken – Wrottesley Park – Nurton – Trescott – Seisdon

Distance: 6.5 miles

Map: O.S. Pathfinder Sheets 891 Wolverhampton (North) and 912 Wolverhampton (South)

Start: Codsall Railway Station

Access: There is a regular daily train service from Wolverhampton. There is also a frequent daily bus service from Wolverhampton bus station to Codsall.

Codsall

The old Codsall, which existed until after the Second World War, has been overwhelmed by the large housing developments stretching out from Wolverhampton, barely bridged by a piece of Green Belt. The place had a reputation for its nearby nurseries and in particular the cultivation of Russell Lupins.

The growth of the settlement came, however, with the Great Western Railway in the last century. This meant that wealthier people could live away from the workplace and commute from leafier settlements. The process does not seem to have stopped at Codsall. It is, however, a convenient starting or setting down point for the walkers on the Staffordshire Way.

Accommodation and Refreshment:

There is limited accommodation in Codsall but you will find shops and public houses in the town. There is a public house in Seisdon.

Seisdon

The area around Seisdon has been subject to much opencast quarrying as it is rich in aggregates deposited during glacial times. The village was once known for its court which was originally held in The Seven Stars inn. Nowadays Seisdon is very much a dormitory village where people travel to work in the West Midlands.

Almost joined to Seisdon is the smart village of Trysull with its village green and maypole, church and splendid Georgian homes.

The Walk

(1) Descend steps from Codsall Railway Station to turn left under the bridge carrying the Shrewsbury line. At the junction go right by Station Villas up a track towards Springfield Hall. The track narrows after the entrance to the hall, climbs up and then descends gently by houses in the village of Oaken. At the junction turn left by a telephone kiosk and then next right into Shop Lane.

(2) Walk along this lane to the main A41 road. Cross here and walk up steps to a stile. Go over it and turn left to walk to the corner by a bungalow, a spot that gets rather wet in Winter. The path turns right to follow the field's edge, around a pool and then 100 metres or so turn left through an old kissing gate into a wood. The path crosses a sleeper bridge and wends its way right through wet ground to a wide green swathe of grass between houses on the right and a golf club house on the left.

(3) The path passes to the right of the club house to a drive (not one immediately on the right to Wrottesley Court). Before reaching the corner go left over a stile, then turn right. A track curves right at the corner but you keep ahead towards and oak tree and onward to a small plantation, through what was part of Wrottesley Park. This area used to be in orchard. Fruit is cropped hereabouts for local markets. Cross a track and continue ahead alongside the woodland. Follow the green lane forward to join a hedge. Half way along, go

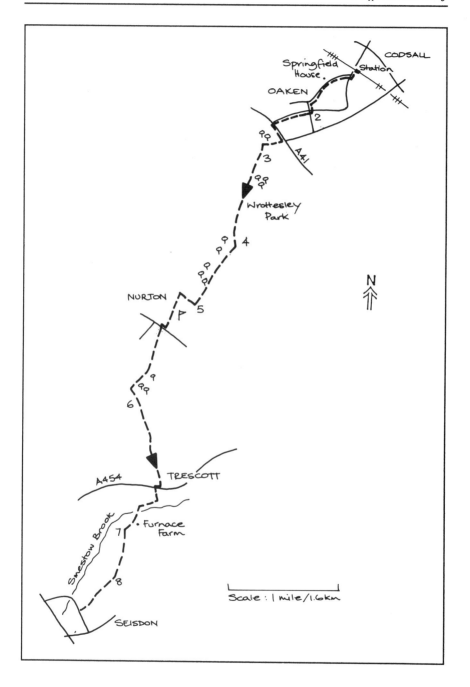

Scale : 1 mile/1.6km

left through a small gate and then right along the other side of the hedge.

(4) Go through fencing and a track heads towards old outbuildings. Before reaching them, go right through a gateway and keep company with a hedge on you right as you walk through rough ground. The path joins a track and at the end of the belt of woodland goes through a gap. Go straight on through the middle of the next field over a gentle brow to a gateway into a golf course, balls flying in all directions.

(5) Go right and follow the perimeter of the golf course to a corner then left along the hedge to a main road. Cross the road and then turn immediately left down a path signposted to Trescott. The bridle-path, which can become nettled in Summer, runs down between pastures to a junction. Cross the track and go over a stile on the right into a field. Follow the path on the left along the field boundary. At the end of the wood, cross a sleeper bridge and stile on the left.

(6) Walk along the wood's edge to join a track. Go right and follow this through fields. It reaches a road by cottages known as Shop Lane in Trescott. At the main road, cross over and turn right for 100 metres. Then go left through a gap into a field by cottages. Follow the field boundary down the field to a stile in the bottom. Cross it and go right through a water meadow near to the Smestow Brook. Walk under the pylons to join a farm track. Turn left and follow it to the outer farmyard of Furnace Farm where evidently evidence of smelting has been found. A lane bears left and the main barn stands ahead. You, however, bear right along a track by the farmhouse garden on the left and cottages to your right to enter a field.

(7) Go along the field's edge to a gap and signpost. Then head slightly left across the next field to a double stile and ahead to another set. Walk straight ahead now towards buildings. Cross the remains of a sleeper bridge in wet ground, with a pool to the right in a trough of the field. Go over the stile by outbuildings and continue to a main track.

(8) Go right here as the track becomes enclosed by fencing. To the left are old quarry workings and as in many other places on this section of route, there are horses corralled too. The track bends left and then right to descend to the distinctive Seisdon House in Post Office Road. Turn right if continuing or left if you wish to visit the village.

SEISDON TO KINVER

Route: Seisdon – Abbots Castle Hill – Highgate Common – Mere Hall – Lutley – Enville – Kinver

Distance: 12 miles

Maps: O.S. Pathfinder maps 912 Wolverhampton (South) and 933 Stourbridge

Access: Seisdon enjoys a bus service from Wolverhampton on Mondays to Saturdays. Seisdon is best approached from the main Bridgnorth road from Wolverhampton. The village is signposted from this road after Trescott. There is limited on-street parking in the village.

Halpenny Green Vineyard

Staffordshire's only vineyard lies just off the Staffordshire Way, one of several hundred vineyards now established in the UK. It has already achieved several awards for its quality wines. The vineyard, which is less than a mile from The Way welcomes visitors.

Highgate Common

The 300 acre common is a mixture of heath and woodland criss-crossed by paths, so it is difficult to pick a route through this haven for birdlife.

The heath amounts to one of the largest tracts in Staffordshire.

Enville

The wooded slopes above Enville Hall descend to parkland surrounding the splendid hall and gardens. While the hall is not open to the public the Staffordshire Way passes nearby and views of parts of

Accommodation and Refreshment

There is accommodation in Kinver. There are public houses in Seisdon and Enville as well as village shops. Kinver has a High Street shopping area, restaurants and a large number of public houses.

the complex can be seen from the path. The attractive sandstone church is a very much restored Victorian building containing many monuments to local landowners such as The Greys, Amphletts and Moseleys. The village itself brings interest for there are three shops almost side by side, one selling clothing, the other groceries, confectionery and the like. Just down the road is the Cat public house which is well known for its food. At the last time of calling it did not, however open on Sundays.

Kinver

Kinver was one of four villages that took part in the Village Enterprise scheme organised by Staffordshire University in the late 1980s. The scheme aimed to develop tourism on terms that were acceptable to villagers. From the project grew the Kinver and District Tourist Association which still thrives many years on. The Kinver Tourist Guides, three enterprising ladies who offer tours of Kinver (on foot or using transport) for visitors, trained as part of the general scheme. Their knowledge is second to none and a tour is firmly recommended. The 'Travellers Joy' information centre also began at the time of the project and bookings can be made here for the guides, accommodation, etc.

Kinver is not new to tourism. It had its own light railway at the turn of the century and this brought thousands of visitors from the West Midlands, especially on a Sunday. The "trams" have gone but the tradition persists for many drive out to sit on or walk along Kinver Edge. In recent years the sandstone cave houses at Holy Austin Rock have been a source of intrigue not only for the interested visitor but for the vandal. Thankfully, this important piece of history is being restored by the National Trust and will be open to visitors.

Kinver also attracts many visitors who are plying their way along the Staffordshire and Worcestershire Canal, a pretty navigation designed by canal engineer James Brindley. Brindley had a house nearby at Brindley Hall, not far from the Staffordshire Way between Enville and Kinver.

There are many fine buildings in the village, some of which have been lovingly restored and are a credit to the community. The Pharmacy and The White Hart pub are distinctive as is the Old Grammar School. Kinver is proud of its heritage and has published several little guides and walks leaflets to interest people. They are invaluable and the authors recommend a weekend stay here just to explore the locality.

The Staffordshire and Worcestershire Canal

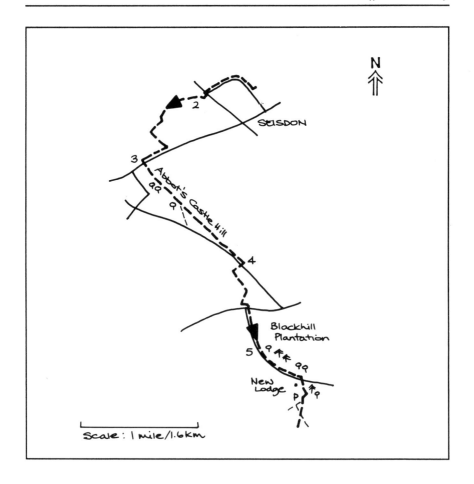

The Walk

(1) From Seisdon House, the route turns right along Post Office Road, a quiet back lane lined with red brick houses. The road bends left and proceeds to a junction. Turn left but then almost immediately right up a track to a junction of tracks. Go right here and pass by a house on your left. The track bends left up the hill to pass by large farm buildings on you right. Over the fields are even bigger farm buildings of factory proportions.

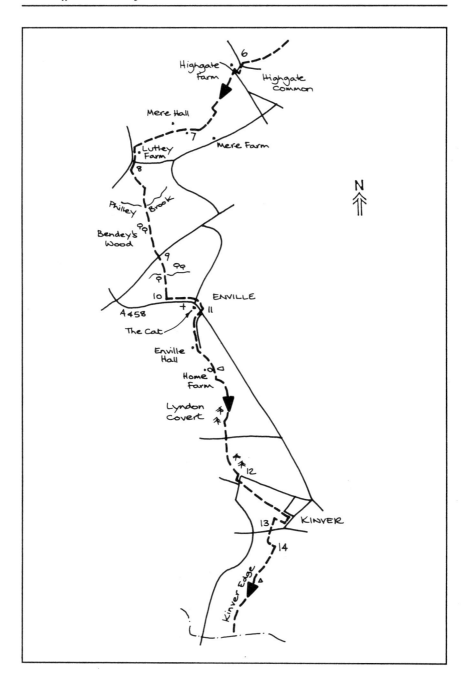

(2) Your path is ahead to a small gate. The path is now corralled along field edges and as with many of the bridle routes in this area, including sections of the Staffordshire Way, the surface is churned up and more difficult to walk during Winter months. Cross a stile onto a narrow lane and turn left. This soon comes to a junction where you bear right to climb up to Abbot's Castle Hill.

(3) A little path eases off to the left before a white house. This bridleway runs along the wooded edge. Keep ahead on the main path which runs near to the hedge on the left for the most part through bracken, bramble and scrub, a favourite hiding place for foxes. There is a fork where a path runs down on the right but ignore this route to the road below. You eventually come to a verge by the roadside.

(4) Cross the road and walk down the track. At the point where a line of electricity poles crosses, turn left and walk ahead along the field boundary, thought to be the route of a Roman Road. You shortly cut right to a track running alongside a fence and quarry buildings where sandstone is being extracted. The track leads up to a road. Go left and immediately right to pass by horses grazing in the field on your left and Blackhill Plantation and a golf club beyond.

(5) Beyond the summit the road descends gently until a left-hand bend by a house known as New Lodge. Go right here along a rutted track to a car park on Highgate Common. Bear slightly left through the car park to walk along a wide track, where cars are stopped by a low level pole. Walk until you reach a major junction where you turn left and then at the next go right, crossing another track and ahead along the fringe of clearing. Join a track to bear left but then within ten paces go right, as signposted, along a lesser path which curves right. This widens again and continues ahead to a junction of tracks. Just beyond where the track rises to a car parking area and road there is a marker indicating that your way is along a narrow path on the right. This soon bends left to run alongside the perimeter of the wood to reach a road by Highgate Farm.

(6) Go left but at the junction turn right and after a cottage on the left, turn left along a tractor track through fields, where there is an entrancing view of Heaton Hall near Bobbington, sparkling white on

a summers day. The track dips to go through a gap and turns left along the next field to a corner where it continues right. The path passes near to Mere Farm with its half-timbered section; it runs down to a hollow pasture which is fenced off, and during wetter months flooded, justifying the name 'mere'.

(7) Cross the track and climb up to walk along a causeway between two pools. To the right stands Mere Hall, a Georgian house, unusually for these parts with a home orchard alongside. The path passes by the orchard along another fenced section and proceeds through two fields to a road near Lutley Farm. Go left and pass the farm. Keep ahead at the junction and turn left down a track by a house.

(8) The track leads into a large pasture. Keep company with the hedge on your left to the field corner and then bear right to a stile. Cross here and walk ahead towards the next corner but just before cut left down a bank over Philley Brook. The path rises to the adjacent field corner. Keep ahead with the hedge and Bendey's wood to your right, ignoring stiles on the right. The Way continues ahead along a hedge beyond the wood to exit onto a road.

(9) Cross over and follow the boundary ahead to the edge of a wood. The path drops down in the corner of the field to a moss-covered bridge which can be slippery when wet, so cross with care. You then proceed up a green lane a white gate leading into an enlarged garden where a notice asks you to keep to the path and follow the markers (none of which were evident when the authors came wandering by). The route follows the right-hand fence up to the main A458 road, something of a shock after all of those out-of-the-way paths and back lanes.

(10) Turn left to follow the roadside into Enville along the verge, although it is debatable as to which side of the road offers a safer passage. You soon reach Enville church. The road passes Enville's shops, a rare mixture of antique shops, general stores, post office and clothes shops standing cheek by jowl at the road junction. Pass The Cat public house, a rare sight on this section of The Way. The Cat has a good reputation for food and ale but be warned – it is not, **repeat not,** open on Sundays.

(11) After the Cat turn right through a car parking area to walk along a road to Enville Hall. Pass by the fine looking buildings on the right and a sport pitch on the left to walk through a gateway (rather than a stile on the right). The track continues ahead to pass by a pool lined with alders below Home Farm. The sunken track continues ahead, where moss covered sandstone holds secrets of a by-gone age. This track winds its way through the bottom edge of Lyndon Covery passing by a bear cage. It rises to a road. Cross over to follow another but narrower thoroughfare, which climbs up through woodland to a bend in a road.

(12) Go right and beyond the house look for a stile on the left into the wood, by a road junction. The path runs through the wood uphill at first then descending to a stile and into a pasture. Head slightly right to the group of houses. Kinver church stands behind as a landmark which can be seen for miles around. The path passes unceremoniously ahead between houses to Windsor Crescent. Turn right to walk along the pavement and at the next junction go right up Meddens Lane. After the last house, go right into the wood and then left as signposted up a well-worn path that leads to a barrier onto a road again.

(13) Cross here and just to your left is an information board referring to the history and restoration of the Rock Houses. You might well be tempted to walk back down to Kinver High Street from here and call it a day. For those seeking a view from the Edge you need to continue up the steps. This is a considerable climb but at the top a panorama opens up across Staffordshire, Shropshire and the West Midlands which makes it all worthwhile, hopefully. The view-finder to the left marks key landmarks.

(14) Some might like to complete the entire Way by turning right on the top along a very wide and well walked track. Pass by a trig point, and keep ahead to the County boundary. This is officially where the route terminates! Such boundaries have little meaning for the walker, however, and the significance of this last section is that it links with the North Worcestershire Path and The Worcestershire Way. Perhaps, you might like to leave these for another day.

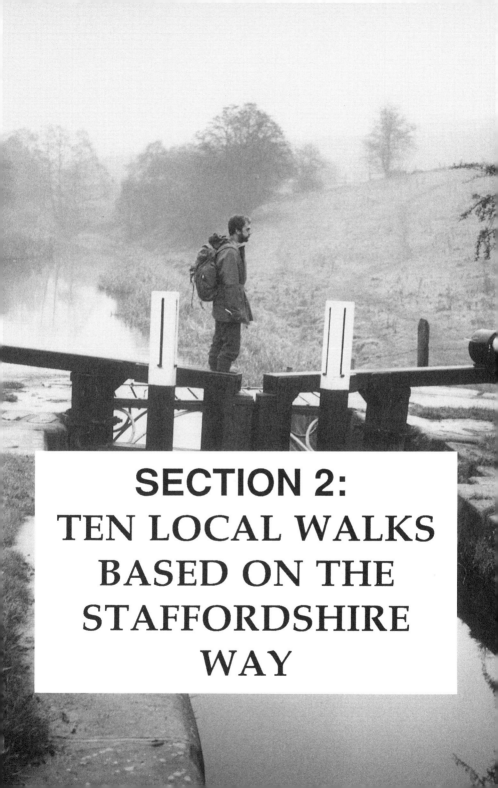

SECTION 2:
TEN LOCAL WALKS BASED ON THE STAFFORDSHIRE WAY

1. MOW COP

Route: Mow Cop – Roe Park – The Bank – Mow Cop

Distance: 3 miles

Map: O.S. Pathfinder Map 792 Kidsgrove and Leek

Start: Mow Cop Folly

Access: Mow Cop is served daily by bus from Hanley. Those travelling·by car should travel on the A34 to Scholar Green where the road to Mow Cop is signposted. There is a car park at The Folly in Mow Cop.

The Walk

This walk drops down the edge of the Cheshire Plain, offering great views on the way. You can discover the origins of Primitive Methodism and explore the old village of Mow Cop. There's quite a climb on the return section but if tackled at a steady pace, the walk is not onerous.

(1) Looking towards the monument, bear slightly left as signposted on the Mow Cop Trail. The path climbs between heather to a track and exits within a few metres onto a road. Go right then cut off left,almost immediately, along a track between buildings. This curves to the right to pass the Old Man of Mow on the right. The seventy foot pillar of gritstone was left standing by quarrymen and is said to resemble the look of an old man. The views across to Cheshire are exhilarating.

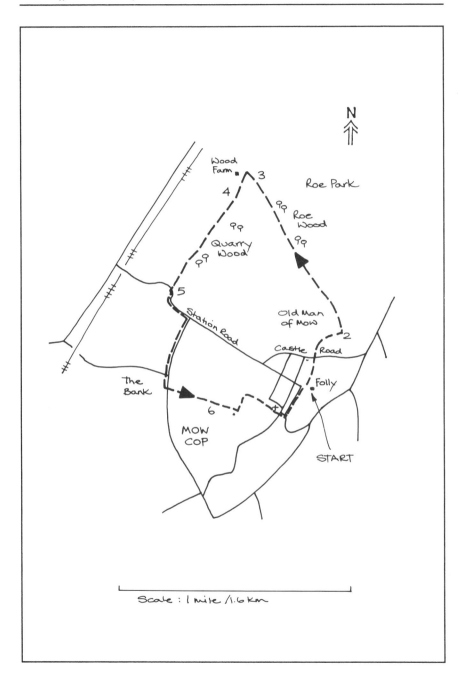

N

Wood Farm
3
4
Roe Park
99 Roe Wood
99
99
Quarry Wood
99
5
Station Road
Old Man of Mow
2
Castle Road
The Bank
Folly
6
MOW COP
START

Scale : 1 mile /1.6 km

(2) Continue along the track past a house and at the corner, where it bears right by a large metal gate, turn left down a narrow path through rough ground. The route is well used, crossing two stiles and fields before entering Roe Wood. It then winds its way down the hillside through hollybushes to turn left before a drystone wall to a gap. The path now enters a field, heading slightly left at first then curving right down the hillside. It passes a farmstead standing to the right and continues slightly right to a gate and then a track.

(3) Proceed down the hill towards a junction but just before look for a stile and signpost on the left. Cross the stile and walk through a small enclosure with Wood Farm on the right. The path winds its way beneath a tunnel of holly bushes and between brambles to pass by a building made of corrugated iron. Just beyond is a stile, which leads into a meadow.

(4) Keep ahead by the water troughs and the path soon reaches a small stream and stile. Cross both and proceed ahead as the path runs through the bottom of Quarry Wood, by a ditch and fencing on the right. It exits by way of a stile and another small winter stream. Walk through the field to cross another stile and then proceed along the track to Station Road.

(5) Cross the road and go left to walk up the road as it bends to a road junction. Turn right to walk along Birch Tree lane, although this seems to be almost devoid of birch trees. At the next junction turn left and walk a short section on the left before turning left into The Brake, a track between houses. As this bends right keep ahead along a green track, once a waggonway from Mow Cop to the Macclesfield canal and railway.

(6) This runs straight up to join a track by a bungalow. Go left but before houses look for a clear stepped path to the right that leads up to the village by the Primitive Methodist Memorial Chapel dating from 1860 and enlarged in 1882. This chapel was pre dated by a smaller place of worship. If you walk to the left into Primitive Street, stone tablets can be seen on the chapel wall indicating the existence of an earlier building dating from 1841.

(7) To return to Mow Cop monument walk by the post office, noting the curious little spring in the wall with the inscription: "Keep thyself pure . . . The Parson's Well 1857". Turn left after the post office into High Street, at one time the scene of Primitive Methodist camp meetings, which attracted tens of thousands to this little quarrying settlement.

A lone walker at Mow Cop

2. BOSLEY CLOUD

Route: Timbersbrook – Acorn Lane – Gosberryhole Lane – Bosley Cloud – Cloud Side – Timbersbrook

Distance: 3 miles

Map: O.S Pathfinder 776 Congleton

Start: From the car park at Timbersbrook

Access: There is a local service from Congleton but it is infrequent. Check details with Cheshire Bus on Crewe 505350. By Car: Travel on the A34 to Congleton then the A527 towards Biddulph. At Mossley crossroads go left on the road to Rushton Spencer and climb out of town. Look for a turning on the left by the Coach and Horses public house signposted to Timbersbrook.

The Walk

Many a walker will contest that late October and early November are the best times to ramble on The Cloud when the air is fresh and the mid afternoon sun softens the landscape beneath your feet. This walk begins at Timbersbrook car park for the climb to Bosley Cloud, an impressive table top hill with magnificent views across several counties and to Wales. The paths are clear enough on the three mile trek but be prepared for a climb to the summit and take care not to venture too closely towards the edge as there is a considerable fall.

(1) From the entrance to the car park in Timbersbrook turn right and walk along Weathercock lane. The Staffordshire Way is joined and, shortly, houses are passed on the left. Go next right up a delightful track adorned by oaks and known appropriately as Acorn Lane. This brings you to the Bosley Road.

(2)Cross over to Gosberryhole Lane, a track leading up the hill towards Bosley Cloud. Note the little indent in the wall with a fresh spring flowing from the fields. The lane climbs up through birch woodland, opening up at a corner to offer a view over Timbersbrook to Congleton Edge and Mow Cop.

(3) Follow the lane as it bends left and continues to rise. There is a well-worn path leading slightly left and passing a National Trust sign. The path continues along the hillside and up to a wood. Keep left rather than entering the wood and follow the hillside path

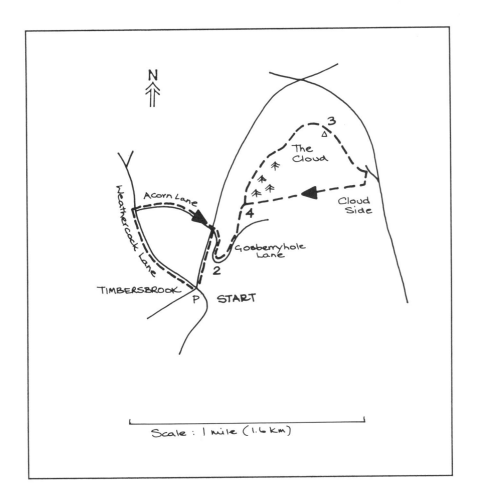

between heather and bilberry to the summit where there are rocky outcrops. On a good day you will see Jodrell Bank and Manchester, the Wirral and the Clwydian mountains. In the foreground is the prominent railway viaduct and nearby Bosley Aqueduct, built with stone hewn from The Cloud. The edge has been quarried throughout the ages leaving oddly shaped rock formations, one of which is known curiously as Bully Thrumble.

The impressive view from Bosley Cloud

(4) Pass by the triangulation point and begin to descend gently, with views to the left to Bosley village and reservoir, with the telecommunications tower on Croker Hill beyond. Directly ahead are The Roaches, Rudyard Lake and Hanley in the distance. The path now tumbles down steep concrete steps to a lane. Turn right and walk up the rise to the bend. Keep ahead here to cross a stile but once in the field go right, keeping company with the drystone wall on your right. At the far end cross a stile into the wood. The path continues

straight on here, keeping near to the drystone wall which is now to your left. It emerges at the wooden gate posts passed earlier.

(5) Regain the outward route down Gosberryhole lane to the road and turn left to walk down to Timbersbrook where a little path leads off right to the car park and picnic area.

3. RUDYARD

Route: Rudyard Old Station – Rudyard Lake – Rea Cliffe Wood – Rudyard Lake Dam – Rudyard Old Station Car Park

Distance: 5 miles

Maps: O.S. Pathfinder Maps 792 Kidsgrove and Leek and 776 Congleton

Start: From the Old Railway Station car park, Rudyard.

Access: Rudyard is difficult to get to by bus, the nearest being the 201 service to Poolend on the main Leek road. Car travellers should travel on the A523 Leek to Macclesfield road bearing left at Poolend as signposted for Rudyard. The car park is on the left immediately beyond the railway bridge. Look out for pedestrians.

The Walk

Rudyard is a firm local favourite. The human endevours of our ancestors to create a reservoir to supply water for Calden Canal has considerably enhanced the scenic beauty of this attractive location.

(1) Start the 5 mile ramble from the old Rudyard railway station. Not much remains of the former buildings, although the Rudyard Lake Railway, a miniature train running along the south eastern shore, now commences from here regularly at weekends (and other days in the summer). Follow the tracks along the linear walkway to reach a point parallel with the reservoir dam. Rudyard Lake was built in the latter part of the eighteenth century as a feeder to the Caldon Canal, one of the earliest and largest constructions of its kind. It is hard to believe that this natural looking lake was built for water supply. There was a steamer on the Lake a hundred years ago and the Rudyard Lake Steam Boat company has reintroduced a service century later!

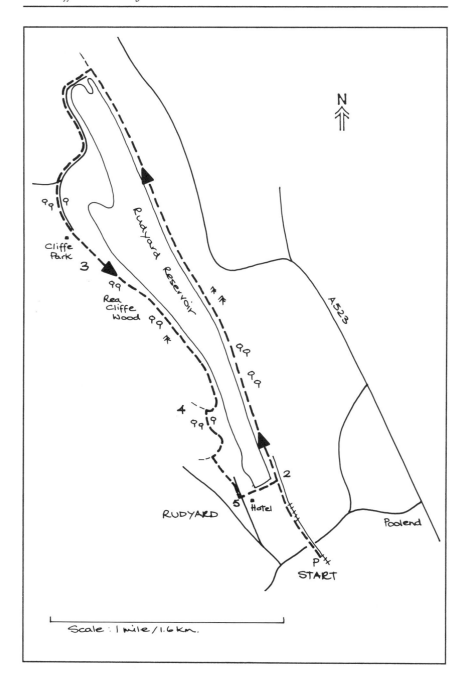

Scale : 1 mile / 1.6 km.

(2) Continue for approximately two miles along the old trackbed to join a dusty track used by fishing enthusiasts passing the site of an old halt here known as Rudyard Lake station, built especially for recreational use. The path comes to a junction by an over bridge. Turn left here and follow the metalled lane around the reed fringed head of the lake. The lane bears left by summer houses and you proceed ahead through a stile by a gate part way along it. The road then curves right up the field to a junction. Take the left fork and pass through a little wood. The track then curves left to pass by Cliffe Park, an impressive looking house built in the 1830s.

(3) Continue ahead into Rea Cliffe Wood and by the sailing club. The track bends right away from the lake, but be vigilant here for your way is shortly to the left (as signposted Staffordshire Way) along a path through scrub and beneath a bungalow. Meet a track and walk through a wood. The track turns right again from the lake by houses. As this begins to rise, turn left down a little path which borders a caravan site. It meets a track and runs behind houses to a road. Go right but before the entrance to the car park of Hotel Rudyard, go left down a path to the dam.

(4) Walk across the southern end of the lake to retrace your steps (to the right) along the old trackbed or you might cheat a little and catch the train back. The residents of Rudyard might not relish the prospect of becoming a premier resort once more but there's a certain feel about these parts which will entice the visitor back time and time again.

4. ALTON

Route: Alton – Saltersford Lane – Townhead – Alton

Distance: 2.5 miles

Map: O.S. Pathfinder 810 Ashbourne and Churnet Valley

Start: The Lock Up, Alton

Access: Alton is served by buses from Hanley (although sometimes a change is required at Cheadle) and Uttoxeter. Travel by car on the A52 road to Cheadle, then follow the signposts for Alton. There is limited on street car parking in the village.

The Walk

It sounds undignified to start from the on-street cell in a village that is tranquil nowadays, especially when the nearby theme park is not in full swing. This easy ramble takes to the quieter parts on the periphery of all excitement.

(1) From the Lock Up in Alton, sitting judiciously on the corner of Dimble Lane and Smithy Bank, cross the road and walk up Lime Kiln Lane. As this bears right at a junction with Hurstons Lane, cross the latter and go through a stone gap stile into a field. Continue ahead away from the village to cross a stile. Once over go ahead in a smaller enclosure which leads to a stile which exits into the old salt route known as Saltersford Lane.

(2) Turn left and walk along slabs as the lane can become exceedingly wet in winter. It dips gently and as you see a house ahead go left over a stile, not immediately seen, into a field. Walk up a sunken path, presumably once a cart-track, with Fareglow Farm on your right. Cross a stile into another green lane and turn right. Your way is through the gateway, and you then turn left to cross a stile in the

next boundary. There's a good view across the Churnet Valley from here to Alton Towers, the rides being well-hidden in the extensively wooded park.

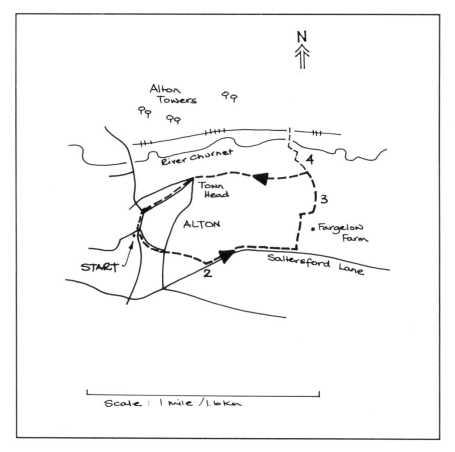

(3) Walk ahead for 50 paces then cross a stile on the left. Head across the field in the direction of Alton Towers. In the opposite boundary there is a small wooden stile that leads down a steep hillside to the valley bottom. You might wish to choose this route. You can then cross the bridge over the Churnet and turn left along the old trackbed to return to Alton railway station.

(4) However, on this occasion the walk remains at high level. Do not cross the stile but strike out slightly left across the field to a stile by a gate. Keep ahead in a similar direction in the next field heading for the projecting corner in this L shaped field. Then proceed towards the barns of a farm at the end of the village known as Town Head. The path gets very muddy in this vicinity during Winter months as you cross a stile by the gate and onto the road. Turn left and then first right into High Street, which leads back into the centre of the village.

The Lock Up, Alton

5. ROCESTER

Route: Rocester – Abbotsholme School – Havenhouse Farm – Marston Montgomery – Marston Lodge – Rocester

Distance: 6 miles

Map: O.S. Pathfinder Map 831 Uttoxeter

Start: Public Car Park, Rocester

Access: Rocester is served by buses from Ashbourne, Uttoxeter, and Cheadle. It is signposted off the Uttoxter to Mayfield road.

The Walk

This ramble follows paths that are not that well walked. They dip into Derbyshire and return to the banks of the Dove and Staffordshire. The route is easy going except for the occasional awkward stile.

(1) From the public car park turn left to walk along Rocester's main street to pass the Red Lion public house and ahead by flats. Pass the police station and a meadow leading to the parish church. Historians point to an earlier abbey on this site. Just beyond is Rocester Mill, built by Richard Arkwright, the inventor of the Spinning Frame and a great developer of the factory system of manufacture. The mill was built in the years 1781 to 1782.

(2) Cross the Rocester Bridge and walk down steps on the right into fields. The path continues ahead in the first field but, once across the footbridge, bears slightly left to the next stile and bridge. Cross these and Abbotsholme school stands to your left. Cut across the field in a similar direction to another footbridge then head slightly right up the bank in the school grounds heading to a point to the right of the school sports hall.

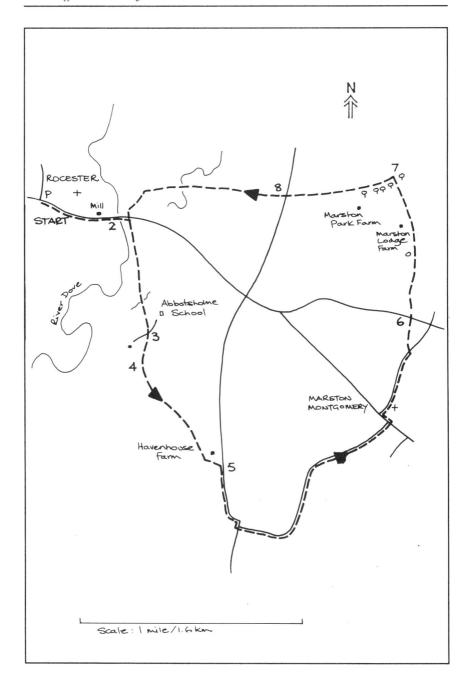

(3) The path exits onto a lane. Cross this and a stile into a field by the hall. Cross the stile to the rear of it and a path leads to a stile into the next field. Head slightly left here to a gateway which exits onto the track again. Go right and pass the entrance to a bungalow. At the edge of the garden cross a stile on the left, and over a temporary fence. Head slightly right up the bank to the top far corner where young trees have been planted. The right of way is not clear here. Local walkers, however, usually climb over the wooden fencing on the left here and turn right to walk to the field corner and then left up the bank to a small gate in the top corner.

(4) Once through continue straight ahead to cross a stile in the next boundary. In the next field, keep ahead with a hedge on the left but, as this bears left, you head right to the far top-right corner. Go through the gap and follow the hedge on the left around to the left to cross a stile in the corner. In the next field head towards the right of the barn belonging to Havenhouse Farm. Join the track and turn left to follow this to a road.

(5) Turn right to follow this road to a junction where you follow the left fork to climb up to the village of Marston Montgomery. Turn left at the first junction then right by The Crown Inn. The road passes to the left of the church, dating from medieval times but restored since. Continue ahead to leave the village and at a corner before a red brick house bear left along a footpath which crosses a stile by a gate. This narrow path soon gives out into a field and proceeds ahead to exit by way of a gap stile onto a road.

(6) Turn right and then immediately left along a track to Marston Lodge Farm. Where this bends left to go through the boundary, head through the field to the right of a pool where a stile by a gate leads to a track, which can be muddy. Follow this as it curves left through a gate but then turn sharp right through an adjacent gate. Follow the hedge on the left now a few paces around to another gateway. Go through here and then keep ahead now with the hedge to your right.

(7) Come to an old gap stile which leads into a woodland belt. Walk through the wood and turn left at the other side. There are great views from here across to the Weaver Hills. Follow the wood's edge down to a stile with Marston Park Farm to the left. Head down a

large field to meet the track at the bottom end. Cross a stile by a gate, go over the road and cross another stile.

(8) Head slightly left to cross another stile mid field by a gate and proceed in a similar direction. Cross a stile by a gate and head for a point just to the right of Rocester church spire. Cross the footbridge and then head similarly to a gap in the next field boundary where the field indents. Follow the hedge around to the left to a stile and then walk up the track on the embankment to a gate which leads onto the road. Turn right to walk back into Rocester.

The Parish Church at Marston Montgomery

6. ABBOTS BROMLEY

Route: Abbots Bromley – Schoolhouse Lane – Hobfield Lane – Bagot's Park – Radmore Fields Farm – Abbots Bromley

Distance: 3 miles

Map: O.S. Pathfinder map 851 Abbots Bromley

Start: The Butter Cross, Abbots Bromley

Access: Access by bus is difficult with limited school and market day services. By car travel on the B road from Uttoxeter. There is limited on street car parking in the village.

The Walk

This is a little saunter along the Staffordshire Way towards Bagot's Wood, the largest remaining tract of woodland in the old Forest of Needwood area, returning through the valley of Ash Brook to the ancient settlement of Abbots Bromley.

(1) The walk leaves the village centre from the Butter Cross along Schoolhouse lane, by the old school and surrounding modern houses. The road continues ahead, dipping down to the chill waters of the Dunstal brook, then rising to a sharp right-hand corner. Keep ahead here along a green track, known as Hobfield Lane, to cross a stile between two barred gates.

(2) The track now becomes a path, following a hedge down to another stile. Cross this and within thirty paces turn right over another stile then left now proceeding with the hedge to your left. The way crosses a stile into the next field, turns left to follow the hedge to the corner then right along the boundary to a stile. Cross here and turn right, following the fields edge on the right into the valley of the Story Brook. The path cuts through a wood and at the

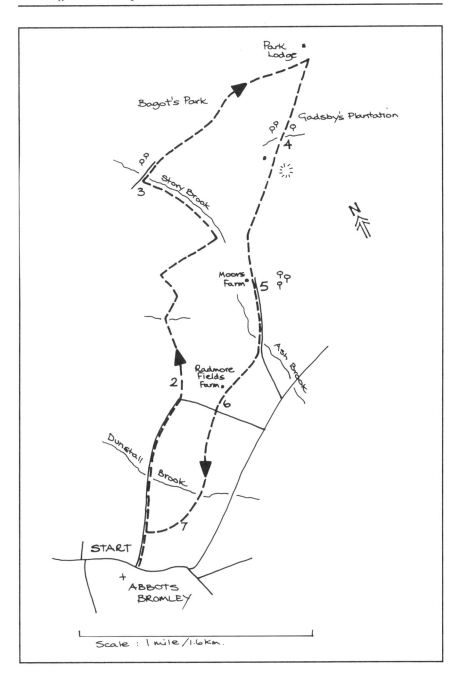

Scale : 1 mile / 1.6 km.

corner it begins to climb gently alongside the brook until a concrete access road is reached.

(3) Go right here to climb up to and through the farmyard and into Bagot's Park, now a sea of large fields. In earlier centuries, this would have been a forest where wild deer roamed. The concrete road continues through Bagot's Park to pass by Park Lodge on the left. At this point be vigilant for your way is to the right over a stile, marked with a small wooden footpath sign. The path follows the curve of the field until a small wood known as Gadsby's Plantation.

(4) Cross a stile and footbridge into the wood. The path then follows the stream for 100 metres before heading slightly left to a stile and into enclosed fields again. Keep ahead, passing by a house on the right and then old workings to the left, before joining a track by way of gates in a coral. Turn left along the track and shortly pass Moors Farm.

(5) The track becomes a metalled road and dips to Ash Brook and a wood on the left. Look for a stile on the right. Cross this and walk ahead through a patch of nettles, seemingly as fresh in winter as summer. Keep close to the hedge on your left and just beyond Radmore Fields farm on the left there's a stile on the left. Cross this and climb the bank up to another stile leading onto an access track.

(6) Walk ahead to cross the road and straight on again. A stile leads into a pasture, with a view of Abbots Bromley ahead now. Cross the next stile and then turn left by the water trough over another stile before bearing right down the bank. The well-worn path leads across the lovely little valley to a footbridge over the Dunstal Brook. Head diagonally right up the bank to a gap and then ahead in a similar direction where a stile by a gate leads to houses.

(7) The path curves right onto the residential road which leads to Schoolhouse Lane. Go left at the junction to return to the village, well known for its traditional horn dancing ceremony which takes place every September, for its handsome houses and for its welcoming inns about the marketplace.

7. SHUGBOROUGH

Route: Great Haywood – Shugborough – Punch Bowl Car Park – Colwich – Great Haywood

Distance: 5 miles

Map: O.S. Pathfinder Maps 851 Abbots Bromley and 850 Stafford
Start: The Clifford Arms, Great Haywood

Access: There is a daily bus service from Stafford to Great Haywood. Those travelling by car should travel on the A51 to Great Haywood, turning right for the village as signposted. There is limited on street car parking.

The Walk

This is one of the loveliest walks in the book, taking in the parkland of Shugborough, the wooded hillsides of Cannock Chase and the tranquil beauty of the Trent and Mersey canal.

(1) Start the 5 mile ramble from The Clifford Arms in Great Haywood. Turn right to walk by the post office and traditional cottages along Trent Lane. Pass beneath the arch of the railway bridge and across the Essex Bridge into Shugborough, home to the earl of Lichfield and now administered by the County Council on behalf of the National Trust.

(2) The path now proceeds ahead through the Shugborough estate, along a narrow lane enclosed by fencing. On the right is the hall, a splendid building which is open to the public at certain times. The lane joins a wider access road to pass by the farm and lodge, the former also being open to the public. Across the parkland, on the hillside, is the Triumphal Arch, modelled on the Arch of Hadrian in Athens. The access road veers to the right but you continue ahead on a lesser track to cross the railway and onward to the main road.

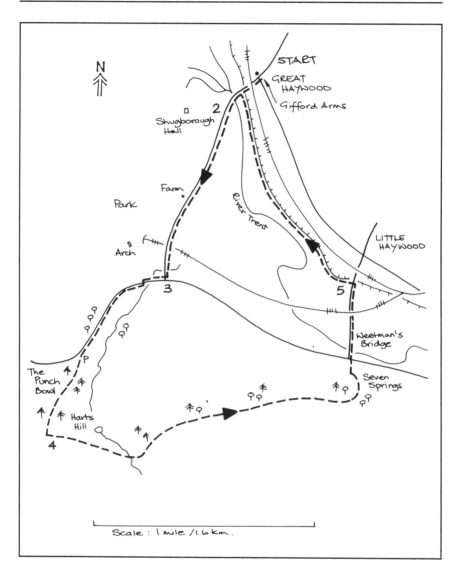

(3) Turn right to walk along the pavement, but this gives out shortly, so cross over to walk along the grass verge on the other side of the road. Your route reaches Punchbowl car park. Enter the parking area and walk up the main track which climbs away from the car park into woodland.

(4) The path soon drops to a junction at Harts Hill, in Cannock Chase. Go left here and follow the track to a prominent ford with stepping stones. Turn left to cross the stream, then climb up between wood and bracken hillsides for nearly one mile to Seven Springs, ignoring turns to the left and right. The track descends more steeply and bears slightly left to go through the car park. Follow the track to exit onto the main road. Cross with care then continue ahead along a road over Weetman's Bridge and beneath the railway towards Little Haywood.

(5) The road reaches the canal where you join the towpath and turn left to walk the remaining mile along the Trent and Mersey canal back to Great Haywood.

The Mansion House, Shugborough

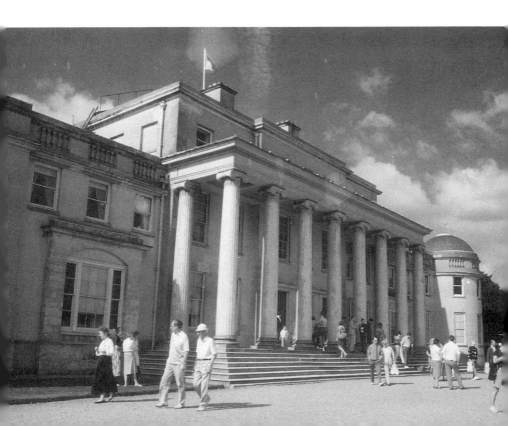

8. PENKRIDGE

Route: Penkridge – Cuttlestone Bridge – Congreve – Whiston Mill –
Preston Vale – Penkridge

Distance: 3 miles

Map: O.S. Pathfinder 871 Cannock North

Start: Penkridge Church

Access: Penkridge is well served by trains and buses from Wolverhampton and Stafford. Travel on the A449 from Stafford. There is car
parking off the main road.

The Walk

This ramble takes you through gently undulating farming county,
typical of mid-Staffordshire to a former mill, now a private residence.

(1) Start the ramble, which is mainly on quiet back lanes, from
Penkridge church. The path enters the main entrance to the churchyard then proceeds to the left of the church into a pedestrian tunnel
beneath the railway line. It then exits onto the access road to the
Hatherton Hotel. At the junction turn left along the road towards
Water Eaton. At the next junction, go right to cross the sandstone
Cuttlestone Bridge over the River Penk. Soon, you turn left along a
quieter lane to Congreve, a hamlet that was once the home of a
famous Staffordshire family of the same name, including writer and
philosopher William Congreve.

(2) Look for a track on the right after Congreve farm, a bridleway
signposted to Preston Vale. Before the gateway to Congreve Manor,
an early eighteenth century building of character, go right up a green
way. The track curves to the right and then leads into a field with
fine views to the right of Penkridge church and Cannock Chase. Go

through the gap in the next boundary and proceed ahead as the hedge on your left curves away. Walk diagonally left across the field towards a wood.

(3) Go through the gate into the wood with a dried-up pond to the left and a pool to the right. This little path, flanked by nettles, leads to a small gate by a barn. Go through it and then turn left along a track by the farm buildings, passing through two gates and along a

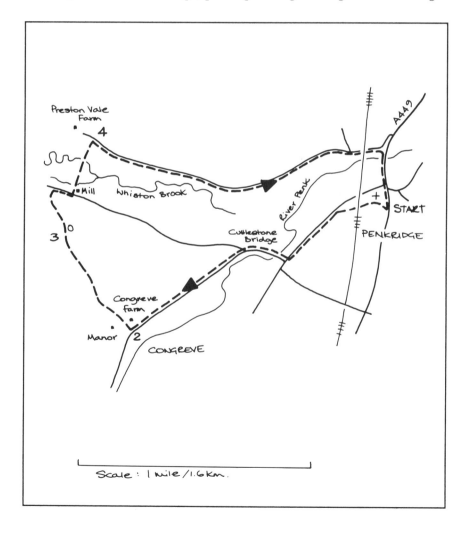

track down to a road. Turn right here but just before the drive to Whiston Mill (now a private residence) go left along a path between fence and hedge to a gate. Go through this and then head slightly right to a footbridge over the Whiston Brook. One wonders how the brook provided a sufficient head of water to power the old mill. Continue straight on to the houses of Preston Vale.

(4) Once on the lane, turn right to return to Penkridge where the road joins the main A449. Turn right for the centre and church.

The weekly market at Penkridge

9. SEISDON

Route: Seisdon – Abbots Castle Hill – Trysull – Seisdon

Distance: 4 miles

Map: O.S. Pathfinder Map 912 Wolverhampton (South)

Start: The Seven Stars public house

Access: There is a limited bus service from Wolverhampton on Mondays to Saturdays. Travel on the main Bridgnorth Road from Wolverhampton. The village is signposted after Trescott. There is limited car parking in Seisdon so please park considerately.

The Walk

The walk leads to the ridge bridleway of Abbots Castle Hill before descending through fields to the pleasant village of Trysull.

(1) From the entrance to the Seven Stars public house, turn left to join the Staffordshire Way, by turning left onto a track before meeting a T-junction. Follow the route instructions shown in the Route Guide on pages 74 and 75 (i.e. line 3 of paragraph 1, plus paragraphs 2 and 3).

(2) Having joined the road at the end of Abbots Castle, Hill Ridge, bear left and follow it for 100 metres. Then turn left through a gap in the hedgerow signposted as a path.

(3) Keep ahead, using the middle electric telegraph pole as a marker. Go through the gap, cross the track and then go slightly right to go through a gateway into a large field with the hedge to the right. Go through a gap into the next field and then keep ahead in the next equally large field. There is a pool and farm to your right. Go through another gap in the far corner and turn slightly right, then ahead along a green lane. When you see the houses at the end of the

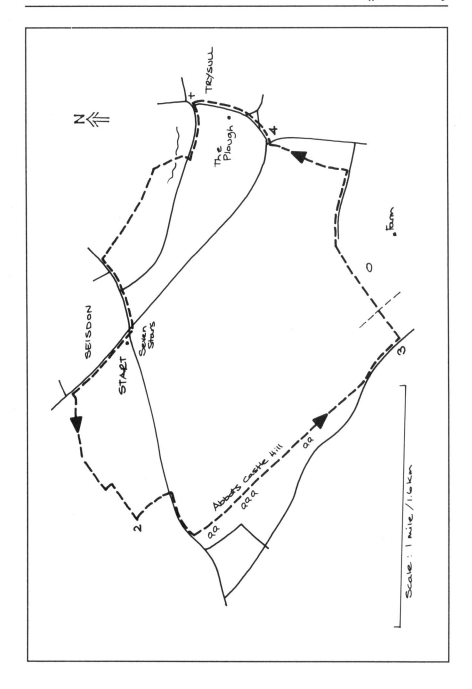

N ⟸

TRYSULL

+

The Plough •

4

• farm

0

SEISDON

Seven Stars

START

3

Abbots Castle Hill

aa aa aa aa aa

2

Scale : 1 mile / 1.6 km

lane, at the end of a group of bushes look for a gap on the left (stile requested). Follow the hedge on your right to a gap, which leads to a triangular junction on the Feiashill Road.

(4) Walk ahead to cross the junction and follow the road as it bends left to pass The Plough public house then onwards to All Saints church surrounded by a group of fine houses. Turn left onto the Seidon Road and at the outskirts of the village leave the road by a stile to cross the stream. Climb up the bank, crossing stiles, to soon enter a green lane. Turn left and follow this through to a metalled road in Seisdon. Turn left to return to The Seven Stars public house.

The Parish Church, Trysull

10. KINVER

Route: Kinver – Stewponey – Hyde Farm – Kinver

Distance: 4 miles

Map: O.S. Pathfinder Sheet 933 Stourbridge

Start: Travellers Joy on the High Street

Access: Kinver enjoys a daily bus service from Stourbridge. Kinver is signposted from the A449 road south of Wolverhampton. There is car parking in the village.

The Walk

The walk follows the High Street to the Staffordshire and Worcestershire Canal, an area where there would have been mills during the last century. One survived until the 1970s.

(1) From the entrance of Travellers Joy turn left to walk along High Street and out of the village. Pass the ornate waterworks building on the left belonging to the South Staffs Waterworks Company. On reaching the Worcestershire and Staffordshire canal turn left onto the towpath at Bridge Number 29, opposite the Vine public house.

(2) Follow this along a delightful stretch of canal sharing the valley with the River Stour to Stewponey Bridge passing, along the route, Hyde Lock, where Hyde Mill once stood nearby. Go left to leave the canal up to the old trackbed of the Kinver light railway, a thriving concern at the turn of the last century. Cross the main road to a pavement and walk up to a point opposite to the entrance to Stourton Castle, a building of character which stands on the site of buildings that date back hundreds of years.

(3) Your way is to the left here, through a kissing gate and then heading slightly right over the field to another kissing gate at the

wood's edge. Go through the kissing gate and walk down steps, then
ahead through woodland. Proceed through a gate and beneath a
group of remarkably tall trees that are appealing in all seasons. Keep
ahead through a gateway with a garden and house to the right.
Continue ahead until a track is reached.

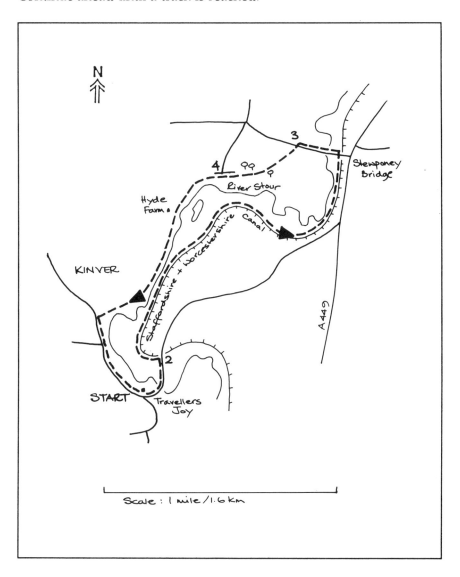

(4) Go left and then ahead along a narrow path by a house with the River Stour to the left and the old track of the light railway. The path is corralled at first, then goes through a riverside plain to a kissing gate which leads into a sports playing field. Pass to the left of the Community Centre and walk up the drive to the main street. Turn left to walk by a rare outlet of Bathams beers, the Plough public house, and back to Kinver's Tourist Information Centre, 'Travellers Joy'.

Tall trees, near Kinver

USEFUL INFORMATION

ATTRACTIONS

Staffordshire has many attractions which appeal to the visitor. Some of them lie on The Staffordshire Way, such as Shugborough Hall or The Rock Houses at Kinver and have been mentioned in the main text of the book. There are other places of interest not far from the Way which you might wish to visit when taking a day's break from walking. A number are listed below (from North to South of the route):

Grange Gardens, Biddulph

The re-opened Victorian gardens at Biddulph Grange lie two to three miles off the Mow Cop Trail section of the Staffordshire Way. The gardens were created over a twenty year period from 1840 onwards by the Bateman family and a friend with great skill and flair, Edward Cooke. The house and gardens were sold to Robert Heath in the early 1870s and he continued to enhance both gardens and the house. In 1923 the premises were bought by a Health Authority and remained as a hospital until the late 1980s when Staffordshire Moorland District Council coordinated a restoration programme. The gardens are now administered by the National Trust. An admission charge is made. Bakers' Coaches run a special recreational service to the gardens from Hanley.

Biddulph Grange and Gardens

Little Moreton Hall

"Happily reeling and somewhat disorderly" is how Pevsner described this marvellous half-timbered structure surrounded by moat and
trees. In the hands of the National Trust, Little Moreton Hall is open
to the public. Recent restoration has included a Knot Garden. Little
Moreton Hall stands about three miles from the Staffordshire Way,
near Mow Cop.

Little Moreton Hall (Chris Rushton)

Brindley Mill

Brindley Mill is on Macclesfield Road, Leek. It is a celebration of the canal and mill engineer who once worked here. The water-powered corn mill has been restored to working order and is a fascination in its own right. Brindley was nothing less than a genius and is particularly famous for his design of the Harecastle tunnel on the Trent and Mersey Canal near Kidsgrove. Unfortunately, Brindley's life was cut short when he developed pneumonia after getting soaked whilst surveying the Caldon Canal at Froghall. He is buried at St James Church in Newchapel. The Mill is run by a Mill Trust and a small admission charge is made.

The Potteries

The uniqueness of the six towns which make up the Potteries is the multitude of pottery manufacturers in such close proximity. Many offer factory tours and even more have factory shops which attract visitors from all over the world, not only to world-famous names such as Minton, Royal Doulton, Spode and Wedgwood but also smaller companies which specialise in different ware. The China Link service (Bakers Coaches) offers a guided hop-on/hop-off tour around the shops and City attractions on Mondays to Saturdays including Bank Holidays.

A demonstration in the Visitor Centre at Wedgwoods

Alton Towers

For many, this is the best theme park in the UK. The exhilarating rides are undoubtedly appealing to young people but do not overlook the exquisite gardens laid down for the Earls of Shrewsbury in the last century. The gardens are often open during spring and late autumn when the rides are shut, and are well worth the detour from Alton Village. If you happen to be walking as a family, this stop is essential for younger members and good fun for mums and dads too!

Stafford

Stafford is the county town and a possible cut-off point for a few days walking (by catching the bus into town from Great Haywood). It has a pleasant central core around the Ancient High House, the largest timber-framed house in England, dating from the 16th century. That's where you will find the Tourist Information Centre. There are several attractions nearby, including Stafford Castle and Izaak Walton Cottage at Shallowford.

Weston Hall and Park

Situated on the Shropshire border, near Brewood, this fine historic house has exceptional collections of paintings, porcelain and silver. There are also attractions throughout the park and gardens.

USEFUL READING

Other publications of particular interest to walkers include:

"Staffordshire Walks, Simply Superb", Les Lumsdon, Sigma Press, 1990.

"Pub Walks in North Staffordshire", Les Lumsdon and Chris Rushton, Sigma Press, 1993.

"The Staffordshire Village Book", the Staffordshire Federation of Women's Institutes, Countryside Books, 1988.

"Shire County Guide Staffordshire", Peter Heaton, Shire Publications 1986.

STAFFORDSHIRE CUISINE

Staffordshire has developed its own regional specialities and, if you're keen to try them, several local publications contain recipes. You can also find recipes for such delicacies as Trentham Tart, Lobby and – as featured on this page – oatcakes, in "A Pint-Sized History of Stoke-on-Trent" by Joan-Ann Grindley (also published by Sigma Leisure).

Master Oatcake Maker – Les Lightfoot

The Oatcake

Several small oatcake bakers remain in North Staffordshire to supply local shops and pubs with this regional speciality snack. The oatcake once formed the basic diet of the farm worker and potter alike, a filling meal when times were hard and lunch breaks short. Made with oatmeal, fresh yeast, a hint of sugar, salt, water and whey or milk, this underrated product is often eaten at breakfast with eggs and bacon or beans. Oatcakes can be found on the menu at pubs and cafes in the area, delicious when hot and filled with cheese, tomato or bacon. You can also buy an oatcake mix at some shops to take home!

STAFFORDSHIRE BREWS

The giant brewers Bass and Allied have stand almost opposite each other in the brewing capital of England, Burton-upon-Trent. They are well represented in Staffordshire pubs, including those to be found along the Staffordshire Way.

There are other brewers, however, that have fought in recent years to secure a sufficient number of outlets for their rather tasty brews. It is no mean task to survive in a market place dominated by the big brewing combines. Therefore, small brewers rely very heavily on pubs which are genuinely free of tie and willing to offer customers a wider choice. If you are fortunate, you might chance upon beers from one of three small-scale Staffordshire breweries:

Burton Bridge
Telephone: (0283) 510573

This brewery company survives under the very noses of the giants in Burton upon Trent. Established in 1982, it brews several bitters, a porter and a Winter dark beer known across the bar as "Old Expensive". There is a 'brewery tap' in Bridge Street, Burton and these fine brews are available in several free houses.

Rising Sun
Telephone: (0782) 720600

The range of beers - "Rising", "Setting", "Sunstroke" and "Total Eclipse" reflects the strengths of the beverages brewed at the Rising Sun Inn at Shraley Brook to the west of The Potteries. They certainly bring a little sunshine into your life.

Titanic
Telephone: (0782) 823447

Named in honour of Captain Smith from Burslem, the brewery now serves an increasing range of free houses, including the Black's Head in Stoke-on-Trent, a real treat for those who enjoy a good pint. Titanic Brewery now has its own pub, The Bull's Head in Burslem market place.

Explore the countryside with Sigma!

We have a wide selection of guides to individual towns, plus outdoor activities centred on walking and cycling in the great outdoors throughout England and Wales. This is a recent selection:

PEAK DISTRICT DIARY – Roger Redfern
An evocative book, celebrating the glorious countryside of the Peak District. The book is based on Roger's popular column in *The Guardian* newspaper and is profusely illustrated with stunning photographs. *£6.95*

I REMAIN, YOUR SON JACK – J. C. Morten (edited by Sheila Morten)
A collection of almost 200 letters, as featured on BBC TV, telling the moving story of a young soldier in the First World War. Profusely illustrated with contemporary photographs. *£8.95*

There are many books for outdoor people in our catalogue, including:

RAMBLES IN NORTH WALES
– Roger Redfern

HERITAGE WALKS IN THE PEAK DISTRICT
– Clive Price

EAST CHESHIRE WALKS
– Graham Beech

WEST CHESHIRE WALKS
– Jen Darling

WEST PENNINE WALKS
– Mike Cresswell

NEWARK AND SHERWOOD RAMBLES
– Malcolm McKenzie

RAMBLES AROUND NOTTINGHAM & DERBY
– Keith Taylor

RAMBLES AROUND MANCHESTER
– Mike Cresswell

WESTERN LAKELAND RAMBLES
– Gordon Brown

WELSH WALKS:
Dolgellau and the Cambrian Coast
– Laurence Main and Morag Perrott

WELSH WALKS:
Aberystwyth and District
– Laurence Main and Morag Perrott

– all of these books are currently £6.95 each.

For long-distance walkers, we have several books including:

THE GREATER MANCHESTER BOUNDARY WALK
– Graham Phythian

THE THIRLMERE WAY
– Tim Cappelli

THE FURNESS TRAIL
– Tim Cappelli

THE MARCHES WAY
– Les Lumsdon

– all £6.95 each

This is the start of our series of cycling books, available now:

OFF-BEAT CYCLING & MOUNTAIN BIKING IN THE PEAK DISTRICT
– Clive Smith (£6.95)

MORE OFF-BEAT CYCLING IN THE PEAK DISTRICT
– Clive Smith (£6.95)

50 BEST CYCLE RIDES IN CHESHIRE
– edited by Graham Beech (£7.95)

CYCLING IN THE COTSWOLDS
– Stepehn Hill (£6.95)

Available June 1993:

BY-WAY TRAVELS SOUTH OF LONDON (£7.95)
– Geoff Marshall

Available October 1993:

BY-WAYS BIKING IN THE CHILTERNS (£7.95)
– Henry Tindell

We also publish:

A fabulous series of 'Pub Walks' books for just about every popular walking area in the UK, all featuring access by public transport

A new series of investigations into the Supernatural,
Myth and Magic

Superb illustrated books on Manchester's football teams

– plus many more entertaing and educational books being regularly added to our list. All of our books are available from your local bookshop. In case of difficulty, or to obtain our complete catalogue, please contact:

Sigma Leisure, 1 South Oak Lane, Wilmslow, Cheshire SK9 6AR

Phone: 0625 – 531035   Fax: 0625 – 536800

ACCESS and VISA orders welcome – call our friendly sales staff or use our 24 hour Answerphone service! Most orders are despatched on the day we receive your order – you could be enjoying our books in just a couple of days.